Environmental Politics
in France

Environmental Politics
in France

Brendan Prendiville

Westview Press

BOULDER • SAN FRANCISCO • OXFORD

Copyright © 1994 by Westview Press, Inc.

Published in 1994 in the United States of America by Westview Press, Inc., 5500 Central Avenue, Boulder, Colorado 80301-2877, and in the United Kingdom by Westview Press, 36 Lonsdale Road, Summertown, Oxford OX2 7EW

Originally published in French under the title *L'Ecologie, la politique autrement?* in 1993 by L'Harmattan

Library of Congress Cataloging-in-Publication Data
Prendiville, Brendan
  Environmental politics in France / by Brendan Prendiville.
    p.   cm.
  ISBN 0-8133-8822-8
  Includes bibliographical references and index.
  1. Environmentalism—France—History.   2. Environmental policy—France—History.   I. Title.
GE199.F8P74   1994
363.7'00944—dc20   94-16017
                                                                      CIP

Printed and bound in the United States of America

  The paper used in this publication meets the requirements
∞ of the American National Standard for Permanence of Paper
  for Printed Library Materials Z39.48-1984.

10   9   8   7   6   5   4   3   2   1

To my mother and in memory of my father

Contents

Tables and Figures

FIGURES

Preface

"We're all green now" was the title the well-known journalist R. Cans gave to his recent book (Cans 1992). Environmentalism in France is in fashion and everybody wants a piece of the action. Industry uses it as a sales pitch (e.g. Peugeot promised to plant a tree in the region of Brittany for every car they sold in 1992) and politicians of all sides have understood its vote-catching appeal.

In the field of science, the environment has been a research interest for some time. René Dumont (agronomist) has been warning the West of the state of third world countries since the 1930s and is already a living legend among French environmentalists. In Sociology, Alain Touraine studied the anti-nuclear movement in 1980 (Touraine 1980) and Edgar Morin has popularized the notion that we need to "environmentalize" our thinking and to forge a new "paradigm" of the environment (Morin 1990, 1993). In Philosophy, Cornelius Castoriadis traced an ecological path in 1981 (Castoriadis and Cohn-Bendit 1981), Michel Serres drew up the 'Natural Contract' in 1990 (Serres 1990) and, recently, Luc Ferry asked some daunting questions about the 'New Ecological Order' (Ferry 1992).

So, are we marching towards greater awareness of the links between social and natural problems? Or will environmentalism fade away like exhaust fumes in the wind?

Brendan Prendiville

Acknowledgments

When books are being written, life goes on. My first thoughts at the end of this exercise are, therefore, for Babeth.

My thanks also go out to Rebecca Donnellan, Fiona O'Connell and Dominic Fitzgerald for their precious corrections and comments. On the technical side, without the help of the Ecole Nationale Supérieure des Télécommunications de Bretagne in Rennes, France, this endeavour would have been even more arduous. I would, in particular, like to thank Joëlle Le Bruno, Patrice Conil and Patrick Pondaven for their patient help and advice at crucial moments. Finally, a special thanks goes to Armelle Cavret for her help and encouragement over the years.

B. P.

Introduction

Environmental politics[1] in France, as elsewhere, is an attempt to balance out the relationship between human beings and nature. To bring man (and woman) back down to earth, as it were. To take him off his cultural pedestal and plunge him back into a natural world of which he has always been an integral part:

> Mankind has to stop acting like a kind of Gengis Khan of the solar suburbs and consider himself not as a shepherd of life, but as a co-pilot of Nature". (Morin 1990: 92)

Human beings are social beings. Banal as this statement may be in Sociology, it is fundamental to any understanding of human activity. At the beginning of the industrial era, the French sociologist, Emile Durkheim, expressed concern about the weakening of social relationships and the dangers of individualism. We will never know how he would have judged today's increasingly atomised Western society but his initial concerns were not far removed from those of contemporary environmentalists who wish to rebuild the social and natural environments. Why rebuild? Firstly, because over the last twenty-five years the natural environment has begun to show signs of wear and tear due to pollution. Secondly, because the social environment is becoming increasingly divided into first and second class citizens who make up the 'dual society'; i.e. those who are integrated into society and those, increasingly numerous, who are excluded from it (e.g. homeless, jobless etc.).[2] Environmental politics in France is about making the links between (natural) pollution and (social) exclusion. How much emphasis is given to the natural or social side of the environmental coin depends on the period and the militants themselves, as we shall see.

This book will draw a picture of environmental politics in France; from what was seen as a "vast social movement" (Simonnet 1979: 121) to what has become an electoral force. We will do this by studying four of its facets: its history, political culture, ideology and social base and typology. We will trace the path of French environmentalism and the obstacles it has encountered from the beginning of the 1970s to the early 1990s; two decades of extra-parliamentary activism, of political organisation, electioneering and ideological frenzy. These two decades have witnessed many changes both in the nature of the environmental movement and the society of which it is a part. Both aspects will be considered.

In Chapter 1, we will show how environmental politics has evolved from a nebulous mass into two political structures (*Les Verts* and *Génération Ecologie*) struggling for a place in political society. In order to facilitate understanding of this evolution, we will refer at times to the two axes of the environmental movement. The vertical axis concerns political society (i.e. institutional politics) and the horizontal axis involves the extra-institutional activity within civil society. The scope of the horizontal axis is very wide as it can range from active participation in an anti-nuclear campaign to tending an organic garden plot. Environmentalists also meet other social actors within this axis who have similar aims (e.g. associations, third world activists, regionalists etc.) and distinguishing the different parts is not always easy. The two axes are, of course, a purely theoretical construction as the two constantly overlap in practice. We shall see, however, that during the two decades in question, one has alternately dominated the other and we shall attempt to explain why.

Chapter 2 looks at the political culture of French environmentalism by considering a series of related questions. What is the nature of the national political culture within which French environmentalists are forced to operate and how has this context affected them? What are the myths, symbols and references of French environmentalism? Do the political and cultural practices of its activists and sympathisers correspond with its discourse? What is the importance of environmental identity and to what extent are the concerns of environmental activists reflected in it? Environmental activists are often seen as nature conservationists even though they consider social and natural issues indistinguishable. In this second chapter we will begin to see why.

Chapter 3 concerns environmental ideology. To be more precise, the different sources of the environmental belief system will be analyzed in this chapter. Few movements enjoy being labelled as 'ideological' and environmentalism is no exception. Despite this semantic reticence however, there is, of course, an ideological content to the environmentalists' belief system and we shall see that it stretches from the extreme-left to the extreme-right. Just how long it can retain such ideological breadth is an open question but such diversity goes some way to explaining the conflict which has often been visible between activists.

The final chapter discusses the idea of a social base for environmentalism and presents a typology of activists and sympathizers with a view to answering the following questions: Is the gender divide an equal one? Is there a turnover of activists? How important is religion? What do environmentalists do for a living? Where do they live and what is their level of education? How much do they earn and what form of social commitment do they prefer? Chapter 4 is principally quantitative and allows the reader to see the changes in the typical environmental activist between 1983 and 1990.

Notes

1. The terms 'environmental', 'environmentalist' and 'environmentalism' are used in this book as English translations of the French terms appertaining to the area of politics now known as 'green politics'; i.e. *écologiste, écologie politique, écologisme*. The term 'conservationist' is used to designate those apolitical organisations concerned with nature protection.

2. The dual society within Western societies is often compared by environmentalists to the dual society on a world level between rich (North and West) and poor countries (South and East).

1

The History

In this chapter we will trace the history of French environmentalism. In the lively 1970s, it was a diffuse movement and "culturally (...) extremist" (Boy 1981: 400). During a decade of wider opposition to the right-wing President Valéry Giscard d'Estaing, it joined forces with other new social movements which sprung out of May 1968 (e.g. feminists, regionalists, consumers etc.) for whom institutional politics was to be avoided at all costs. This was a time of street demonstrations and extra-parliamentary activity during which any electioneering was purely an exercise in biodegradable politics. The following decade began with a search for the 'alternative society' before giving way to a gradual electoral institutionalization.

Fertile Ground

The French environmental movement can be traced back to the first conservationist association founded by Isadore Geoffroy Saint-Hilaire (*Société Impériale d'Acclimatation*). Today's FNE (*France-Nature-Environnement*), the FNSPN (*Fédération Nationale des Sociétés de Protection de la Nature*) of 1969 and the SNPN (*Société Nationale de Protection de la Nature*) of 1958 are each a part of this conservationist strand of the environmental equation which changed little until the first signs of water pollution became apparent in the 1950s. In 1962, the first opposition to nuclear power was manifested by a certain Jean Pignero when he created the association, APRI (*Association pour la Protection contre les Rayonnements Ionisants*) in reaction to compulsory X-rays for children and nuclear testing.[1] The same year heralded the first press campaign against pollution by the journalist Pierre Pellerin in journals such as the *Bêtes et Nature*, *Guérir*, *Toute la Pêche*, *Le Monde* and *La Vie*. In 1965, Jean Dorst, Professor at the Natural History Museum in Paris, published his book, *Avant que la nature meure* and two years later, the *Torrey Canyon* oil spill hit the English and Breton coasts, affecting the public environmental consciousness for the first time.

1968

The influence of the events of 1968 on environmentalism has been noted by different commentators[2] and, indeed, it would seem a fundamental reference point in any understanding of the new content and forms of political expression that the environmentalists have tried to institute. The first signs of popular discontent of a qualitative nature are to be found at this time as the concept of 'environmentalism' took over from that of 'conservationism', as critiques of the consumer society drew closer to those concerning industrial pollution, as the radical critique of daily life previewed the environmentalists' rejection of "tomorrow's paradise" (*les lendemains qui chantent*). If environmentalism is a product of the "western plethora of the second half of the twentieth century" (Simonnet 1979: 124), the premisses to environmental analyses concerning the need for a healthy civil society[3] can be traced back to the students' movement of May 1968 and its demands for greater autonomy. To take one example in the realm of urban environmentalism; the first signs of protest concerning the wastage and pollution of individual transport, as opposed to collective transport considered to be less wasteful, could be seen with the creation of the association, *Fédération Nationale des Usagers des Transports* (FNAUT), in January of the same year.

Elections and Organizations

With regard to electoral progress, the first environmental candidate to stand in an election was at Mulhouse (Haut-Rhin) in March 1973 for the legislative elections of that year. It was no surprise that this first campaign took place in the east of France, given its geographical position placing it at the heart of Europe and leaving it open to influences from other countries. In the event, the candidate received as large a share of the vote as the PSU,[4] setting the stage for a long rivalry between the alternative left and the environmentalists.

In March 1971, the French branch of the Friends of the Earth (*Amis de la Terre*) was created and was soon to become a central pillar of the environmental movement. The originality of this organization was that it had a 'foot' in both the vertical and horizontal axes of environmentalism. That is to say that it considered working for change in political society (e.g. elections, organization of political structure) and civil society (e.g. associational life) to be equally important. In November 1982 it decided to concentrate on civil society while others concentrated on political society (see below 1982 - 1989) but during the 1970s it was to be very much in the environmental forefront organizing actions such as the popular bike demonstrations against the inner Parisian two-lane highway in the early 1970s. It was also to become the springboard of Brice Lalonde's[5] political career.

Activism

The 'Vanoise' Affair. With regard to what could already be called environmental activism, this post-1968 period was fertile. In 1969 the first major environmental struggle was to take place. The project of building a ski resort in the Vanoise National Park,[6] albeit strictly illegal, was given the go-ahead sparking off a massive reaction (500,000 protest letters). The campaign was led by a journalist (Jean Carlier) who had created the AJEPNE (*Association des Journalistes et Ecrivains pour la Protection de la Nature et de l'Environnement*) a year earlier, and was supported by the newly-created FNSPN (*Fédération Nationale des Sociétés de la Protection de la Nature*).[7] Together they were successful in putting a stop to the project and furthering the political consciousness of many hitherto apolitical conservationists.

Nuclear Power and Non-Violence. The first major anti-nuclear demonstration in France was organized by the CSFR (*Comité de Sauvegarde de Fessenheim et de la Plaine du Rhin*; Bas-Rhin) on the 12 April 1971 bringing together 1,300 people. Three months later, the demonstration against the Bugey nuclear plant (Ain), called for by Pierre Fournier in *Charlie Hebdo*[8] was a surprising success with 15,000 people turning up to bathe in the July sun. Claude Vadrot (Vadrot 1978) remembers that the first signs of a split could already be seen in this demonstration between the 'anarchists'[9] and the 'organizers' in the environmental movement. This split was to widen over the years.

Two months before the Bugey demonstration, the battle between the small farmers of the Larzac plateau (Aveyron) and the French army was just beginning. The army wished to extend an already existing camp which would have involved evicting several farming families. This struggle between the agricultural 'David' and the military 'Goliath' became known as the 'Larzac affair' and was soon to become a symbol of non-violent resistance against the military and the State, bringing together different sectors of contemporary political opposition. Environmentalists and pacifists came to promote non-violence and to defend small communities. Certain sectors of the extreme-left came to fight the State and the alternative left party, the PSU, came for a mixture of the two. In May, there was a token demonstration of protest before a much larger meeting on the 6 November when 6,000 people turned up to support the farmers. The affair was to last a decade before President Mitterrand, realizing the powerful political symbol it represented, cancelled the project on his election in May 1981.[10]

Books and Newspapers

Between 1970 and 1974, environmentalism began to make inroads into different sectors of French society. In the field of literature, highly important in France, the first use of the concept of 'environmentalism' was seen in a revised version of J. Dorst's aforementioned book published during the 'European Year for the Protection of Nature' in 1970. The same year heralded the first articles by an environmental legend, Pierre Fournier, in the satirical magazine *Hara-Kiri Hebdo* attacking pollution and the nuclear industry from an environmental, social and, increasingly, political standpoint. He continued in 1972 by creating the anarchist journal *La Gueule Ouverte*, which has remained, along with its creator, one of the most oft-cited references in the environmental movement's early history.

In the year leading up to the first environmental presidential campaign, two new magazines appeared. The first was in the form of an environmental press agency which collected all types of information and then published it on a weekly sheet. The APRE (*Agence de Presse Réhabilitation Ecologique*) was initiated by Jean-Luc Burgunder and its contents often demonstrated the different, ostensibly contradictory strands of the contemporary environmental movement. It was also a reflection of a wish to counter what was seen as a fundamental weakness of the French state; i.e. insufficient public information.[11] In 1977, the APRE became *Ecologie-Hebdo* and is today the longest running environmental magazine, now under the name of *Ecologie-Infos*. The second magazine was the *Sauvage*, which was originally a supplement to the left-wing weekly, the *Nouvel Observateur*. Created by Alain Hervé from the Parisian branch of the Friends of the Earth, *Sauvage* was an interesting venture in that it could be seen as the left-wing reply to the anarchism of P. Fournier. It is equally worthy of note that the eco-socialist philosopher and essayist André Gorz had a weekly column under the pseudonym Michel Bosquet in the *Nouvel Observateur*.

This list of literary sources would be incomplete without reference to Ivan Illich whose numerous works have forged some of the most basic, world-wide environmental concepts. His work, for example, on conviviality and the theory of watersheds in human action has had a fundamental influence on environmental thinking.[12]

Institutions

This period was one which also gave rise to institutional concern over the environment, both nationally and internationally. In France, the Ministry of the Environment and the Protection of Nature was created in 1971 with Robert Poujade at its head. This minister did not take long to declare that such a ministry was the 'Ministry of the impossible' before resigning three years later.

Internationally, the 'Club of Rome' was formed in 1970 by

concerned industrialists, sociologists, philosophers and technicians with a view to inspecting more closely the state of the planet. On the 11 May 1971, a *Message of 2,200 scientists* was published by UNESCO concerning the multiple dangers of the contemporary world (e.g. energy resources, overconsumption in the West and food shortages in the Third World, galloping rises in population and increasing social problems). This message was reinforced by the French publication in 1971 of Paul Ehrlich's book on the population explosion (Ehrlich 1971) and the following year witnessed a milestone with publication of *The Limits to Growth* (Meadows et al 1972) commissioned by the 'Club of Rome' two years previously.

This brief discussion of the historical background to the French environmentalists' first appearance in the public eye during the presidential elections of 1974 gives some idea of its increasing activity. Environmentalism was beginning to take the place of conservationism under the pressure of events, the most important of which had been the 'revolt' of 1968 and the new content and form of political and cultural expression on the part of a generation.

The Crazy Years: 1974 - 1981

The importance of the presidential elections in France is such that they can often serve as a time-lock for the study of social and political phenomena. In the case of the environmentalists, the movement which took shape during the presidency of V. G. d'Estaing (1974 - 1981) was of a different nature to that which followed it into the first presidency of François Mitterrand (1981 - 1988) even if this is not, necessarily, a direct reflection of these presidents' policies.

The seven-year period that was about to open was one in which the environmental movement was dominated by an anarchist tendency, politically and culturally. This was reflected in the desire to 'live out an alternative lifestyle' by participating as little as possible in State structures. Any desire to be participate in the political process was quite weak and limited, between 1974 - 1977 at least, to symbolic electoral participation as a means of airing views. The dominant anarchist tendency[13] was, however, to lose its influence as the more organized elements began to win the debate on strategy. This period can be divided into two overlapping sectors: firstly, the anti-nuclear movement and, secondly, the electoral and structural activity of the environmental movement.

The Anti-Nuclear Movement

The anti-nuclear movement was the spearhead of the environmental movement in many Western countries, during the 1970s. In France, it was particularly impressive in its capacity to mobilize large numbers of people. It was, however, equally impressive for its remarkable lack of success, although the reasons for this are as much a reflection of the political system in which it was forced to operate as any strategical errors it made.

Science as a Political Weapon. The support given to the anti-nuclear movement by different scientific (and legal) institutions was an important factor, as without such support the credibility of its arguments would have been difficult to maintain. This support came from two categories; firstly, those scientists who were actively involved in the wider environmental movement and, secondly, others who quite simply had doubts about the scope of the government's programme. In the first category came the organization *Survivre*, founded in 1970 by the mathematician Alexandre Grothendieck as a French branch of the international organization for the survival of humanity. *Survivre* was to melt into the *Groupe de Scientifiques pour l'Information sur l'Energie Nucléaire* (GSIEN) which, itself, came out of the *Appel des 400 scientifiques*,[14] the latter falling into the second category. This appeal was as much concerned about the technical risks as it was about the lack of democratic consultation before and during the construction of nuclear plants and had collected close to 2,000 signatures by the end of May 1975. From within the nuclear establishment itself there also came support from an ex-director of the CEA, Leo Kowarski,[15] and from the EDF (*Electricité de France*) economist, Louis Puiseux.

These examples of strictly scientific support reflect the scientific activist base that has influenced the environmental movement from the earliest stages of its history. G. Sainteny talks of the "new type of politician with an education in the sciences" (Sainteny 1990: 36) and a cursory look at leaders past and present confirms this. For example, Pierre Samuel, a leading member of the French Friends of the Earth is a mathematician. Philippe Lebreton, the initiator of *Ecologie 78* (see below) and founder member of the MEP (*Mouvement d'Ecologie Politique*), is a biologist. René Dumont, the first environmental presidential candidate in 1974 is an agronomist and Antoine Waechter, candidate in 1988, is a doctor in Ecology.

In the legal and economic domains, the SFDE (*Société Française du Droit et de l'Environnement*) and the IEJE (*Institut Economique et Juridique de l'Energie*) from Grenoble both played a part as vehicles of anti-nuclear discourse in more official circles.

The Periods of Struggle. The seeds of an opposition movement to nuclear power were sown by Jean Pignero as early as 1956 although the anti-nuclear movement only really began at the beginning of the 1970s. The first demonstrations took place, as we have seen, at Fessenheim and Bugey in 1971. In December of the same year there was an international meeting of anti-nuclear activists in Strasbourg with a view to choosing tactics and, even at this early stage, disagreements appeared between the legal reformists and radical activists (Nelkin and Pollack 1982: 58). However, the real impetus for a mass movement was given by the announcement of the 'Messmer Plan', initiated by the French Prime Minister of the same name on the 6 March 1974 stipulating that nuclear power was to produce 70 percent of the country's electricity by 1985. The struggle was underway and the following four years witnessed opposition movements overlapping in intensity. The nuclear 'Bastille', however, was to prove virtually impenetrable.

At Braud St Louis (Gironde) the opposition united farmers, conservationists (e.g. SEPANSO: *Société pour l'Etude, la Protection et l'Aménagement de la Nature dans le Sud-Ouest*) and environmentalists, mainly from outside the village in a running, often pitched, battle with riot police and the EDF. The opposition was not united as certain professional categories who stood to gain by the construction (e.g. shopkeepers) were in favour. The conflict gained national media attention with marches of thousands (1975), a bomb attack on the *Conseil Général*[16] and a sit-in by farmers at the offices of EDF. The town council voted for a five-year moratorium but, at one point, the mayor summed up the role of local representatives by declaring: "I have no power whatsoever in making decisions. Go and see the EDF" (*Ecologie* 1981: 40). This feeling of powerlessness was reinforced when the construction begun before the permit had been delivered. The conflict, which had begun in 1974, fizzled out after 1976 having failed to prevent the construction.

At Flamanville (Manche), the town council (PS: *Parti Socialiste*) was all for the proposed nuclear plant, considering that in a depressed region it would bring work. Between 1974 and 1978, there was a similar scenario of conflict, at times violent, with threats and division (in favor of the plant: workers, the local priest and town councillors; against: farmers, conservationists and environmentalists) which split the local community. One interesting factor in the conflict was the change in attitude between a local referendum held on the 8 April 1975 (435 for, 248 against) and another at the end of 1976 (35 percent for, 65 percent against [Nelkin and Pollack 1982: 71]). In between these two referenda, there had been a strike by technicians, organized by the CFDT (*Confédération Française Démocratique du Travail*), in protest against the claimed dangers of privatization of the nearby reprocessing plant in La Hague (Manche). This strike seemed to demonstrate that there was disagreement amongst technicians on the potential dangers and no doubt explains the change in opinion. This strike was also important in another respect as it represented an important bridge-building exercise between the environmentalists, nuclear power workers and their trade union. Such a collaboration between a section of the working class, albeit principally white collar, and the intellectual classes that make up the bulk of the environmental movement was to virtually disappear during the 1980s, even if the general influence of trade unions also declined in France (see Chapter 4).

Despite the (unofficial) referendum results, work was given the go-ahead on the 8 February 1977, eight months before governmental permission appeared in the form of the *déclaration d'utilité publique*.[17] This alone gives some idea of the legal impunity with which the EDF could act, thereby furthering the feeling of powerlessness on the part of opponents.

In Alsace, the struggle against the proposed nuclear plant had begun as early as 1971 when the first anti-nuclear demonstration took place. No major events happened for the next three years when, in 1974, the EDF began a campaign of information which the CSFR tried to counter, only to find closed doors in the small (900 inhabitants), somewhat conservative, village. The ensuing struggle between the pro and anti-nuclear factions, most of whom were from outside the village, reached its climax in May 1975 when bombs started to go off at the plant on the 25th of the same month. The struggle continued into 1977 with a hunger strike and the 'occupation' of pylons in Alsace built to transport the electricity from the nuclear plant.

The 1977 demonstration in Malville (Isère) marked the end of the first period of the anti-nuclear movement in a dramatic way. It was the third demonstration on the site, bringing together environmentalists from France, Germany, Italy, Belgium, Great Britain and Switzerland, and was the largest ever, up to that time. Malville was to be the site of France's first commercial fast-breeder reactor, *Super-Phénix*. A fast breeder reactor is a very different machine to that of a first generation PWR (*Pressurized water reactor*)[18] and environmentalists considered it to be a major step into the 'nuclear society'. In 1976, 15,000 demonstrators turned up and occupied the construction site.[19] The following year, the regional Prefect (René Jannin) ordered the police to prevent a repetition and the result was one death – Vital Michalon, a 31 year-old primary school teacher from the Drôme region – and a hundred wounded. The reasons for such violence at what was to be a peaceful demonstration were twofold. Firstly, the organization by the different 'Malville Committees' had been heavily infiltrated by sections of the extreme-left (Trotskyists and Maoists) for whom the demonstration, and the environmental movement in general, was a platform for direct confrontation with the State. It was this infiltration, as T. Chafer has pointed out, "combined with what they believed to be the unrealistic position adopted by the environmentalists, that led the PS and

.the CFDT to refuse to take part in the Malville committees" (Chafer 1982: 202 - 220). In the event, a few hundred armed demonstrators appeared amongst the ranks of peaceful demonstrators and the organizers had no control over them.

Secondly, the project of *Super-Phénix* was to be the jewel in the crown of France's nuclear programme and was to guarantee its energy independence for decades to come. As such, all opposition was to be met head on. The aforementioned representative of the State in the region, to a large extent, fuelled the tension by stating that "for the second time Morestel is occupied by the Germans", thereby making reference to the presence of German anti-nuclear demonstrators. The atmosphere was so tense that violence was inevitable.

The significance of Malville on the environmentalists was "traumatic".[20] If not the end of mass mobilization, as the struggle in Plogoff (Finistère) was to demonstrate, it did herald the end of the most activist phase of the anti-nuclear movement. It also marked the virtual divorce between the environmentalists and the extreme-left (Trotskyists and Maoists) over the question of political violence.

The second period of anti-nuclear activity is that which began with the accident of Harrisburg (Pennsylvania, 1979) and ended two years later with the only victory of the anti-nuclear movement; the cancellation of the proposed nuclear plant at Plogoff. Other conflicts did, of course, either break out or continue:

(1) At Golfech (Tarn-et-Garonne), for example, a nuclear plant had been in the pipe-line since 1973 and at the end of 1979 (22 October - 21 December) demonstrations took place during the public enquiry (*enquête publique*). In a local referendum, 83 percent of the population had voted against the plant.

(2) At Cherbourg (October 1979) there was an opposition movement against the transport of Japanese nuclear waste to the reprocessing center of La Hague (Manche).

(3) At Gravelines (Nord) and Tricastin (Drôme), the discovery of miniature cracks in the reactors and the decision, nevertheless, of EDF to go ahead with the loading of fuel prompted the first

joint strike by the CFDT and the CGT (*Confédération Générale du Travail*) over nuclear security (September 1979).

(4) At Chooz (Ardennes) the public enquiry of a proposed nuclear plant produced violent clashes between demonstrators and the police throughout May and June 1979.

(5) In the west of the country at Le Pellerin (Loire Atlantique), several agricultural villages lined up against the proposed power plant between 1977 - 1980. The village of Le Pellerin itself was twinned with the Breton-speaking village of Plogoff, thereby giving regionalist overtones to this often violent conflict.

(6) At Plogoff (Finistère), the final major anti-nuclear struggle was also the only victory over a governmental project. The violence during the public enquiry of January 1980 reached hitherto unscaled heights and F. Mitterrand cancelled the project on his arrival to power in 1981.

These examples, set between 1977 and 1980, illustrate that anti-nuclear activity did not disappear after Malville. In fact, Three Mile Island gave a new impetus to many activists but things weren't quite the same and, Plogoff apart, none of these struggles were very successful.[21] The programme seemed unstoppable and the decision of the newly-elected Socialists to press ahead with it (*Le Monde*, 1 August 1981) was the final nail in the coffin.

Reasons for Failure. The principal reasons for the failure were exogenous to the anti-nuclear movement. That is to say, the political culture and administrative system of France leaves virtually no room for minority views to be heard, let alone influence the debate. The centralization of the French political and administrative system has produced a situation in which there is little tradition of civil society intervening in the political decision-making process and opposition views and movements come up against State bodies almost immediately. The intermediaries between the State and the French citizen do not appear to play a sufficient role in defusing potential conflict by allowing minority positions to be heard and taken account of. This has produced a situation in which the citizen is largely unempowered (*déresponsabilisé*), having little form of protest other than direct confrontation with the State. In their account of the anti-nuclear movements in France and Germany, Nelkin and Pollack consider that:

> The greater impact of the protest in Germany than in France followed less from the characteristics of the movement itself -- a movement often paralyzed by internal schisms over tactics and long-term goals -- than on these points of access within the political system and on the ability of activists to exploit them. (Nelkin and Pollack 1982: 196 - 197)

An example of a point of access would be the law courts which the anti-nuclear movement in France rarely used to any effect given the inability of the courts to counter matters of central State policy such as nuclear power. The intimate connections between governmental political and administrative bodies and the EDF are such that the prevention of construction of a nuclear plant, once work has started, is virtually impossible.[22] Another example is the system of public enquiries which only gave the local population an opportunity to express their opinion once the project had been elaborated by the relevant services in Paris.[23] The reaction of municipal councillors towards major technical projects over which they had no control is revealing in this respect, leaving them with a distinct taste of 'fait accompli'.

Stemming from this is the seemingly endemic lack of official information from governmental and administrative sources. In each of the nuclear conflicts, the anti-nuclear movement was faced with an uphill struggle to lay its hands on the relevant information concerning siting and construction details. This explains that a large proportion of the movement's activity was concentrated on obtaining and producing as much information as possible, from within their ranks and without. It was for this reason also that many of the anti-nuclear committees adopted the name of *Comité Local/Régional pour l'Information sur le Nucléaire (CLIN/CRIN)*.

Another, very important, exogenous factor is the relationship between civil nuclear energy, foreign policy and French military policy. Général de Gaulle was the architect of France's foreign policy of independence which, to this day, is based on the independent nuclear deterrent. The links between civil and military nuclear power are now clear to all and the possible uses of the plutonium produced by *Super-Phénix* are equally so. This intimate link between foreign policy, military strategy and energy production made the task of the anti-nuclear movement even harder.

Finally, the importance of the Socialists coming to power remains a major explicative factor in the anti-nuclear movement's premature demise in the 1980s. The cancelling of both the proposed power plant in Plogoff and the extension of the military camp at Larzac defused large sectors of environmental opposition. The co-opting of opposition leaders into government and administrative office did the same. As an example of this, Huguette Bouchardeau, ex-PSU presidential candidate, became Minister for the Environment and Michel Rolant, the CFDT's influential spokesman for energy, became the head of the newly-created AFME (*Agence Française pour la Maîtrise de l'Energie*). The importance of the arrival of F. Mitterrand to power is fundamental to an understanding of the general demobilization of political opposition in France in the 1980s.

Of a more endogenous nature, the internal conflict within the ranks of the anti-nuclear movement did not help the long-term coordination and organization necessary for effective collective action, especially in such a hostile system. The anti-nuclear movement was torn between its different ideological, indeed philosophical strands; between its anarchist and Marxist, reformist and revolutionary, non-violent and violent tendencies. Between those who wished to use the movement as a platform to overthrow the 'bourgeois State' and those who wished to draw support from all social classes on an issue that affected everyone. These conflicts came to a first watershed at Malville with the parting of the ways between the environmentalists and the extreme-left but ideological differences have continued up to the present day.

Elections and Structures

Given the lack of a unified structure up to 1984, the participation in elections was often spontaneous and ephemeral. The structures that came about to organize them were what was subsequently termed 'biodegradable', in that they never lasted for very long afterwards, nor indeed were they intended to. In this section, the electoral and structural progress of the environmentalists up to and including 1993 will be traced.

At the time of the presidential elections of 1974, brought forward due to the death of Georges Pompidou, environmental structures were thin on the ground. The only real national structures were those of *Les Amis de la Terre* and *Pollution-Non*.[24] As the elections approached, it was therefore not surprising that some of their members and journalists from the AJEPNE went to ask R. Dumont, on 7 April 1974, to stand as the environmental candidate. The latter accepted only on the condition that the 'new left' candidate, Charles Piaget[25] did not stand, giving a clear idea of R. Dumont's anti-capitalist sympathies. An environmental candidacy was considered "politically stupid" by the journalist Jean François Kahn of *Radio Europe 1*[26] to which R. Dumont replied:

> what is actually destroying the ecosystems is the search for profit held up as a law of development. The search for profit implies constant increases in production, most of which is no use to man but to produce surplus stock, surplus value and profit within the capitalist system. Consequently, environmentalism must look for a different economic and political structure. (*Ecologie* 1981: 18)

In these elections, the environmentalists had two aims. Firstly to air views and, secondly, to 'sift out' the environmentalists from the conservationists, i.e. to see how many of the conservationist associations would support the campaign which was led by the agronomist, R. Dumont. The sifting process was rapidly effective. Of those who took an apolitical stance were the major national, umbrella organizations; the FFSPN, the SNPN, the LPO (*Ligue pour la Protection des Oiseaux*), *Comité de la Charte pour la Nature*[27] and a host of minor ones. Among those who supported R. Dumont were several regional associations which were also members of the aforementioned umbrella associations; *Fédération Rhône-Alpes de Protection de la Nature, Nord Nature, Survivre en Champagne, Société de la Protection de la Nature en Loir-et-Cher*, CSFR and certain groups of the SEPANSO. This was the first time conservationists had been forced to position themselves with regard to environmentalism and it showed a clear distinction between the positions taken by the national and regional organizations. The regional organizations gave more support than the national ones and this in itself gave weight to environmental analyses on the importance of the region as a political entity.

The first round results were considered a success (see Table 1.1[28]). As for the second round, the French electoral tradition is for first round candidates to 'advise' their supporters on how to vote. At this time, the now traditional position of environmental candidates to refuse to do this was more difficult to adopt. The left was a long way from gaining political power and the hope placed in it remained strong. R. Dumont himself never hid his left-wing sympathies and the compromise reached was that he would not 'advise' his first round voters but would support the left-wing candidate, F. Mitterrand, in a personal capacity. In the aftermath of the electoral excitement the activists decided to pursue the mobilization by creating the *Mouvement Ecologique* (ME) out of the *Collectif National Provisoire du Mouvement Ecologique* which had organized R. Dumont's campaign. The ME survived until 1978 and was centered in the east of France,[29] the west being virtually absent at this time from national environmental structures.

The next important electoral test came in 1977 with the municipal elections.[30] Since the inception of environmentalism in France, local elections have been considered to be the most significant electoral exercise in that they are the most decentralized and closest, therefore, to people's lives and daily concerns. The *commune* (i.e. municipality), in particular, is seen by many environmentalists as the starting point from which a social base could be built and, as such, the municipal elections are given, in theory at least, top priority.

TABLE 1.1   Presidential Elections 1974

	Votes Cast	René Dumont	Percent
Countrywide results	25,057,571	337,800	1.3

Source: Ouest France, 6 May 1974.

The political composition of different lists around the country revealed the state of debate between the different environmental tendencies in that there were several instances of joint lists with other political groups, principally from the alternative left (e.g. PSU) and/or peace movements (e.g. MAN: *Mouvement pour une Alternative Non-Violente*). This convergence between environmentalists and the alternative left at these elections was a logical outcome of the proximity in action that existed at this time between the 'self-management current' (*courant autogestionnaire*) and environmentalism. For prominent members of the RAT (*Réseau des Amis de la Terre*), the two were virtually synonymous:

> Social movement in France in 1977 is not simply a battle between right and left. Within the left there are anti-statist and anti-productivist forces which, to a large extent, are part of the anarcho-syndicalist tradition; the PSU, CFDT, non-violent movements, regionalists and autonomists, etc. For years these people have been struggling side by side with the environmentalists.[31]

The context of 1977 was also one of strong anti-nuclear struggle around the country and the environmentalists hoped to benefit from this. The results were again considered as more than respectable for a first showing in local elections (see Table 1.2).

Stimulated by these successes, several activists were already looking to the legislative elections of the following year. Ideological splits, however, were beginning to strain the electoral edifice as different conceptions of political action became clearer. When P. Lebreton launched the idea of a national organization,

TABLE 1.2   Municipal Elections 1977

	Votes Cast	Alternative Left/ Environmentalist	Percent
Countrywide results	25,267,592	270,000	1.1
Communes with environmental candidates		270,000	9

Sources: *Le Monde*, 16 March 1977; Sainteny 1991: 78.

which he was prepared to lead, he came up against opposition from a strong decentralizing tendency which wished to practise politics in a different way by avoiding pyramidal structures and leaders:

> The history of the environmental movement has been a long and difficult search of how to build a democratic movement (not with a pyramidal structure and a permanent central office) whilst remaining efficient. Certain pitfalls have been avoided. The environmentalists have understood that an environmental party would be catastrophic and have preferred to link up during collective action (e.g. Malville coordination) or in flexible, national federations (e.g. *Fédération des Amis de la Terre* or the ME).[32]

This refusal to accept central structures reflects the anarcho-syndicalist tradition of French politics which was also visible in the anti-nuclear movement:

> This anarcho-syndicalist tradition frequently resurfaces throughout French history: the revolution of 1848, the Paris Commune of 1871, the mass strikes and sit-ins following the victory of a left-wing alliance in 1936 and the events of May 1968 are all the products of this tradition and the anti-nuclear movement, in its rejection of the established political parties and institutions as a medium through which to express its dissent and pursue its struggle, is the modern inheritor of this tradition.[33]

These two quotes are revealing in that they reflect the presence, and relative strength, of this radical-libertarian tendency within the environmental movement, up to this point in time. This tendency was subsequently to lose much of its influence as the environmentalists invested more of their energy in fighting elections. In this respect, 1978 was a strategic turning point for them as the 'organizers' began to win the battle over the 'radicals'.

The legislative elections of 1978 did, nevertheless, see the birth of a unified structure, *Ecologie '78*, which almost immediately found itself in competition with a newly-created Parisian-based group (*SOS-Environnement*) led by Jean Claude Delarue. Considered to be a right of center environmental group by Vadrot (Vadrot, 1978), this latter group managed to conclude an electoral pact with *Ecologie '78* by forming an umbrella organization *Collectif '78*, which attempted to share out constituencies. Candidates were put up where finances were available and agreement was possible. The subsequent confusion for the voter did not help the environmentalists and the results were disappointing (see Table 1.3).

There are different explanations for these results. Firstly, the presence of an alternative left platform, *Le Front Autogestionnaire*.[34] These elections were an important step in the environmentalists' search for an independent political identity and the rift between it and the alternative left began to widen at this time. Secondly, these elections took place after the trauma of Malville and the results seemed to suffer from it.[35] The effect on many anti-nuclear and environmental activists was such that the prospect of an election campaign was insufficient to mobilize the necessary activism. The third explanation was the apparent lack of unity between *Ecologie '78* and *SOS-Environnement* which dissuaded many prospective voters.

The election campaign of *Ecologie '78* had, however, stimulated interest in electoral politics for the more organized wing of the environmental movement. There was lively discussion as to whether it should spend time and money in fighting elections or whether it should patiently build a movement of social change through collective action and social experimentation. A decision needed to be made as the following year, the European elections were to take place. The RAT was not enthusiastic in investing energy in these elections as it considered that the envisaged minorities list was not evidence of "a movement for real social change" (*Libération*, 2 May 1979, 5

TABLE 1.3   Legislative Elections 1978

	Votes Cast	*Collectif 78*	Percent
Countrywide results	28,098,115	621,100	2.2
Constituencies with environmental candidates		621,100	4.7

Sources: *Ouest France*, 13 March 1978; Ysmal 1986: 15; Sainteny 1991: 78.

November 1979). There only remained the activists of the ME and those 'unorganized' environmentalists to make a decision. They decided in favour and confirmed, in doing so, a burgeoning electoral strategy within French environmentalism.

The European elections are, in theory, the most favorable to minority parties as they are held under a system of proportional representation and organized around national lists which have, therefore, national coverage. In theory only, however, as they are also financially crippling if the 'magic' 5 percent which guarantees the reimbursement of electoral expenses is not attained. The (French) necessity to attain this percentage for each list was considered by the political minorities (i.e. regionalists, feminists, consumers, PSU, MRG,[36] environmentalists) as a means to keep them out of the institutions. To counter this, there were discussions amongst the PSU, MRG and the environmentalists at the beginning of 1979 with a view to forming a common electoral platform which would only be binding up until voting day. It was eventually the environmentalists (*Europe-Ecologie*) who took the decision to go it alone; "Through an instinct of self-preservation of what is a really original, totally novel identity, *Europe-Ecologie* has put a stop to negotiations with these two parties" (*Ecologie* 1981: 136).

The results of *Europe-Ecologie* (see Table 1.4), led by the environmental activist from Alsace, Solange Fernex, were disappointing because they came close to the 5 percent. No seats were won however which irritated *Europe Ecologie* considerably given that in other countries, similar or weaker scores were sufficient to obtain representation in the European Parliament (e.g. *Partito Radicale*, Italy: 3.7 percent = 3 seats). In the same year, the cantonal elections (*cantonales*) took place in which the environmentalists' participation was minimal. The cantonal

TABLE 1.4   European Elections 1979

	Votes Cast	*Europe Ecologie*	Percent
Countrywide results	20,176,135	890,000	4.5

Source: Le Monde, 12 June 1979.

TABLE 1.5 Cantonal Elections 1979

	Votes Cast	Environmentalists	Percent
Countrywide results	10,712,811	49,885	0.5

Source: Le Monde, 20 March 1979.

elections take place every 3 years and renew half of the conseil général (county council). They are difficult elections for minority parties as the proximity of the candidates to their electorate is of prime importance. Experience and clientele-type politics tend to be the by-words in this type of election and established politicians are hard to shift. Traditionally, these elections are given little limelight even though they represent a tier of local government. They are, however, a sure sign of an electoral base for any political party and, at this time, the environmental local electoral base was weak, which explains the poor results (see Table 1.5).

The structuring of the environmental movement took an important step at Dijon (Côte d'Or) on the 25 November 1979 with the creation of the MEP (Mouvement d'Ecologie Politique). This was formed out of the ashes of the then recently-deceased (1978) ME, the activists of Europe-Ecologie, Ecologie '78 and 'unorganized' environmentalists. Its aims were twofold; firstly to transform a nebulous entity of periodic activism and sympathy into a coherent political project[37] and, secondly, to create a recognizable, national pole within the political system. It failed in this for three reasons.

Firstly, and most importantly, as Jean-Claude Demaure confided to us: "(it was) too Parisian, full of apparatchiks[38] and ex-leftists (...) the machine took over and the rank and file lost control of it."[39] The MEP was perceived to practise politics in much the same way as any other political party. When one remembers the importance of the anarchist strand of environmentalism and the reticence of prominent members of the RAT towards centralized structures, the MEP's failure to mobilize large numbers of environmentalists is understandable. This centralist image is no doubt the reason why it had little influence within environmental circles in Brittany and, of its three Breton contacts (François de Beaulieu, Michel Politzer, Jean Moalic) only François de Beaulieu, initially, joined the unified environmentalists in 1984 (i.e. *Les Verts*).

Secondly, the composition was not sufficiently widespread. In the direct elections for half the National Council the activists from the east of the country (Rhône Alpes, Alsace, South East,) and Paris were very much in the majority. The west of the country, and Brittany especially, had few representatives. There were of course members in Brittany but the only person to have had any significant national influence was Michel Politzer. The composition of the study group leaders (*28 Commissions d'Etude*) confirmed this tendency with 66 percent of them coming from Paris and the east/south east of the country.

Thirdly, the MEP was in competition with the RAT and not able to bring environmentalists under one umbrella organization. The RAT was more interested in forging a broad-based social movement of oppositional minorities (e.g. regionalists, feminists, consumer organizations, alternative left). The MEP was more interested in creating a uniquely environmental organization that would assert its independent political identity. In this respect, these two different conceptions of political action heralded the split to come between *Les Verts* and *Arc-en-Ciel* in 1986 - 1987 (see below). The importance of the MEP, which lasted up to November 1982, was to have put the process of building a single organization under way even if it was seen as a competitor to the RAT, rather than as a complement to it.

By the time the MEP was beginning to assert itself, the presidential elections of 1981 began to loom. So, in May 1980, the three main strands of the environmental movement came together in Lyon to discuss the prospect of a single presidential candidate. The RAT, MEP and 'unorganized' environmentalists ('*diversitaires*') decided to unite forces and elect one candidate in June of that year. The candidate chosen was B. Lalonde, the head of the RAT and the form of this internal primary was an interesting example of direct democracy as it was open to any French citizen who wished to participate (*Libération*, 16 June 1980.). In July, the electoral organization, *Aujourd'hui l'Ecologie*, was created to run the campaign which lasted for the next eleven

TABLE 1.6   Presidential Elections 1981

	Votes Cast	Brice Lalonde	Percent
Countrywide results	28,901,025	1,122,445	3.9

Source: Le Monde, 24 May 1981.

months amidst an atmosphere of conflict and recriminations between the supporters of B. Lalonde (RAT) and those of P. Lebreton (MEP). The battle for the leadership was underway.

The results of the elections (see Table 1.6) were satisfactory as they tripled the number of R. Dumont's 1974 vote (i.e. 337,800). However, these elections were to be especially remembered for the victory of the socialist candidate, F. Mitterrand, whose first act in power was to call a general election. Despite the financial constraints involved, *Aujourd'hui l'Ecologie* decided to field 174 candidates from a total of 409 and polled 1.1 percent of the national vote (see Table 1.7). These elections were a turning point for France as well as for the environmental movement. The country as a whole was to undergo a certain measure of political demobilization as the opposition movement to V. Giscard d'Estaing's government disappeared. This had an effect on all types of extra-parliamentary activity. More particularly, the environmentalists found themselves operating under the left-wing which, in the past, had seemed receptive to their arguments. The effect on its evolution and strategy was fundamental.

TABLE 1.7   Legislative Elections 1981

	Votes Cast	*Aujourd'hui l'Ecologie*	Percent
Countrywide results	25,141,190	271,688	1.1
Constituencies with environmental candidates		271,688	3.3

Source: Le Monde, 16 June 1981.

Social Experimentation and the 'Alternative Society'

The practice of social experimentation and the underlying idea of an 'alternative' society have been constant features of environmental thought and practice. The idea of an alternative society was one which broke with a tradition of sudden, violent, top-down revolutionary change so ingrained in French political culture. Instead of social change coming from above (Paris or the party headquarters), it was to be put into practice from below with a view to creating long-term, alternative cultural practices. The development of this idea and practice provides a bridge between two decades of environmentalism (1970 - 1980, 1981 - 1993) and may be divided into three periods, even if the dividing line is never quite so clear: the 'drop-out' period, the 'do-it-yourself' period and the 'integration' period.

'Dropping-Out'

The period following the May 1968 events in France was one in which a certain urban exodus took place amongst disillusioned activists who 'dropped out' of mainstream society to live an alternative lifestyle by setting up communes ((*communautés*) in order to flee the constraints of industrial life. The type of 'communes' that were set up, principally in the south of France, were those of the American-inspired, self-sufficient type. They were both a rejection of productivism and a desire to live out more convivial relationships in a "neo-rural" (Allan Michaud 1989: 104) setting although the preparation for such a lifestyle was, in most cases, insufficient. To a large extent, they were stimulated by one of the founding fathers of French environmentalism, Pierre Fournier, whose desire was to set up a type of 'phalange' similar to those advocated by the utopian socialist, Fourier (1722 - 1837):

> The appeals launched by Fournier for a return to practices were heeded by adepts of a healthy life, organic agriculture activists and by the 'commune' movement. They brought about an urban exodus of disappointed revolutionaries, 'back to the earth' experiences which attempted to create little islands of an ideal, free and anarchist society, far from the civilization of technicians, based on a search for an autarchical and self-managed economy. (Simonnet 1979: 95)

The harsh realities of community life and economic survival brought this first wave to an end by the middle of the 1970s.

'Do-It-Yourself' Environmentalism

The desire to live out an alternative lifestyle did not, however, disappear because of this. It simply evolved into a vaster movement of practical alternatives in an urban as well as a rural setting. In the period 1975 - 1980, the anti-nuclear movement and the apocalyptic warnings of the environmental crisis of the previous five years gave way to a wave of social experimentation, particularly in the field of alternative energy. The discourse on the dangers of nuclear power were deemed to be insufficient and the necessity of supplementing it with viable alternatives seemed indispensable to many environmentalists.

In 1975, the magazine *Sauvage* presented a programme entitled: "kit out the (environment-friendly) society of the future" (Allan Michaud 1989: 122). Around the same time, the magazine *Ecologie* relayed the actions of those groups participating in the campaign to promote solar energy (6% *Solaire*) who refused to pay a part of their electricity bills in protest against the massive investment in nuclear energy by EDF. The influence of theories of 'alternative technology' which had been imported from the USA and Great Britain were beginning to be felt at this time and gave rise to an interest in practical applications. Soft technologies, as opposed to the hard technologies such as nuclear energy, became a means of putting theory into practice and the example of solar energy techniques (e.g. house architecture, heating systems) was the most common.

It was also at this time that the second wave of communities began. In the opinion of Léger and Hervieu, these communities were of a different kind: "The utopian community had disappeared, or almost, and had been replaced by the environmental dream of a green, healthy and authentic life." (Léger and Hervieu 1985: 108)

Certain sectors of the organic movement began their itineraries in this wave and this decade was one which resembled, in many respects, the counter-culture of the USA which came out of the 1960s.

Integration

At the beginning of the 1980s, the idea of an 'alternative economy' was coming into fashion.[40] The alternative economy was, and remains, linked to a more general notion of the 'social economy' (*économie sociale*) which can be traced back to the first cooperatives of the nineteenth century.[41] The traditional understanding of the social economy is close to that of the cooperative movement, first put into practice by the Pioneers of Rochdale (GB) in 1844.[42] The 'alternative' activists wished to take this generous concept based on mutual aid and democratic workers' control further by integrating the environmental dimension. An 'alternative' business was seen to be one which "produces a socially and economically useful product, respectful of the environment and natural resources and which is concerned with maintaining a different type of relationship with its clients and suppliers." (Allan Michaud 1989: 33)

In Germany this had already given rise to the *Netwerk Selbshilfe* (i.e. autonomous self-help network) which was created in 1978 and which was enriched by an 'alternative' bank (*ökobank*) in 1985.[43] This German example, among others, inspired the creation of ALDEA (*Agence de Liaison pour le Développement d'une Economie Alternative*) in 1981. According to ALDEA, an alternative economic project is one which brings together four criteria:

(1) *Viability*; that is, the project must be able to balance its budget whether it works in the commercial or social sector and whether its revenue comes from sales or subsidies (i.e. support from the State or from the alternative network). Viability is not, however, considered to be synonymous with profitability. A profitable company is not necessarily viable for the community, if it is polluting or if it exploits the underpaid for example.

(2) *Autonomy*; somewhat vaguely defined, the concept of autonomy for an alternative project centers on individual autonomy at the workplace which would enable him/her to "become his own master and to have greater control of his way of life."[44] Such autonomy should not however prevent the necessary creation of local jobs and the satisfaction of local needs.

(3) *Self-management*; that is, the democratic functioning of the

project based on collective decision-making with regard to production, salaries and conditions of work.

(4) *Solidarity*; that is, solidarity with the less favoured members of the community but also with the alternative network. That is to say, the aim of ALDEA was to create a network of businesses which would support each other and which would have a certain autonomy from the mainstream economic circuits.

The idea of an alternative society has always been an ambiguous one. Alternative in what respect? In working practices? In production choices? In financing? ALDEA attempted to create a network of businesses around the country, one which would have a certain autonomy from the mainstream economy. The reasoning behind such a venture was to create a series of "minor revolutions" which would become so numerous as to "invade the whole of the economy."[45] The least that can be said is that it has had only limited success. On the subject of social experimentation in communes, organic food, renewable energy and recycling, for example, the conclusion is somewhat pessimistic:

> About 750 organic farms, 300 consumer coops, 100 manufacturers of solar energy water heaters, 100 organizations for the promotion of renewable energy -- plus the examples of self-built renewable energy houses [20 to 100] (...) a derisive showing for a movement which was supposed to have deeply penetrated society. (Allan Michaud 1989: 153)

The alternative movement has thrown up more questions than it has answered and, perhaps as a result of its mediocre performance, some environmentalists have questioned the principle behind it. That is to say, is an alternative economy a good thing, given that such an economy would be alongside the mainstream economy and would not, necessarily, modify it? The aim of environmentalism is to modify the mainstream economy by reforming it in a radical way. Such radical reformism (*réformisme radical*) is based on a strategy of creating reforms within the present system rather than creating an alternative to it. This difference in approach could be seen as a reflection of the growing separation in the early 1980s between the vertical axis (institutional political activity) and horizontal axis (extra-parliamentary political action) of French environmentalism.

The expression 'alternative' came into fashion towards the beginning of the 1980s. It replaced the term 'self-management' which had lost much of its meaning given that virtually every political force on the left had laid claim to it. The advantage of the term 'alternative' was to link up theories of 'self-management' with environmentalism. The obstacle was that the former concept was the property of the alternative left (PSU/CFDT) and the latter, that of *Les Verts*. In this respect it could be said that the principal function of the notion 'alternative' has been symbolic. The myth surrounding it has served the purpose of attempting to unite disparate oppositional social and political groupings.[46] These attempts however failed not least because *Les Verts* would not define themselves as anti-capitalist and the alternative left saw such a definition as a necessary premiss. At this point the problems of different political cultures became apparent and when the magazine, *Folavoine*, referred to the alternative movement as "anti-capitalism without a theoretical backbone",[47] it reflected the difficulty of attempting to forge one common political culture from different political traditions, however short-lived.

Practically speaking, there would seem to have been a certain difficulty in creating the desired alternative practices on a sufficient scale. Over the years, the content of the alternative ideal would appear to have changed. From a revolutionary ideal of social and economic experimentation, there has been a process of integration within the State apparatus which has both positive and negative consequences and which highlights the aforementioned ambiguity. The institutional integration allows greater recognition and financing and the budget of ALDEA in 1986 was financed to the tune of 90 percent by subsidies and contracts with State bodies. However, this situation was, and remains, a reflection of the interest shown by the State in the alternative economy as a means of alleviating unemployment. Certain analysts (e.g. Allan Michaud 1989) go so far as to consider that it has served as a vector for the 'dual economy' that took shape in Western societies during the 1980s.[48]

Environmentalism under Mitterrand

Towards an Environmental Party: 1981 - 1984

The aftermath of the presidential elections in 1981 opened up a difficult period for the environmentalists during which different organizations were to lay claim to the 'green mantle'. At this time, the only overtly political organization was the MEP alongside which stood the RAT and, in December 1981, there was the creation of a third organization when certain members of the RAT, *Aujourd'hui l'Ecologie* and of regional environmental associations (e.g. *Fédération Ecologiste du Midi*) created the federally-based *Confédération Ecologiste*. This supplementary creation was a reaction to what was perceived as the MEP's centralizing political practices and of its apparent failure to make any headway in mobilizing new activists. Further impetus was given to the idea of another organization when it became clear that the environmentalists would find no succour within the ranks of the new socialist government, given the latter's decision to continue EDF's nuclear programme in much the same form.[49] The year which followed was one of long and difficult negotiations between the *Confédération Ecologiste*, the MEP and the RAT with a view to forming a single, national organization. These negotiations came to very little for two reasons.

Firstly, the RAT decided in November 1982 to withdraw from the political stage for a mixture of official and unofficial reasons. Officially, it wished to concentrate on furthering the aims of environmentalism within civil society and to leave the building of a purely political arm to others. Unofficially, the RAT had not gained the control it had hoped for within the new *Confédération Ecologiste* at the beginning of 1982[50] which corroborates the comment of B. Lalonde on the process of political unification: "You know, when a movement manages to unite, some people always lose power".[51] The RAT was also worried about the creation of a formal political party having consistently refused to caution this and, finally, it feared losing subsidies if it was seen to be cooperating too closely in overtly political activity.

The second reason concerned the MEP which simply saw these negotiations as a political challenge to its existence as, indeed, they were. Because of this, the MEP simply decided to transform itself into a political party, (*Les Verts-Parti Ecologiste:* VPE) in November 1982. In the same month, the *Confédération Ecologiste* became *Les Verts-Confédération Ecologiste* as both organizations realized the mileage to be made out of the title, *Les Verts.*[52]

This long and difficult year also saw the second environmental appearance at the cantonal elections. There were twice as many candidates but the results differed little from the first outing in 1979 (see Table 1.8) even if the number of votes cast rose slightly (1979: 49,885; 1982: 55,589). However, the following year's municipal elections were eagerly awaited. The environmentalists have always placed greater hope in, and given greater importance to, this type of election as it is considered to best incarnate their slogan; 'Think globally, act locally'. The results were, however, disappointing (see Table 1.9). Compared to the municipal elections of 1977, the vote dropped by half in terms of votes (1977: 270,000) and percentage (1977: 1.1 percent). Times were different, it is true. In 1977, the anti-nuclear campaign was in full swing. This time around, the left was in power and the environmentalists were in open feud. In such

TABLE 1.8   Cantonal Elections 1982

	Votes Cast	Environmentalists	Percent
Countrywide results	12,399,121	55,589	0.4

Source: Le Monde, 16 June 1982.

TABLE 1.9   Municipal Elections 1983

	Votes Cast	Environmentalists/ Alternative Left	Percent
Countrywide results	27,520,144	147,884	0.5

Source: Ouest France, 7 March 1983.

circumstances, the appeal to prospective voters was not all that it should have been.

The Formation and Evolution of *Les Verts:* 1984 - 1989

With the European elections looming large, it was clear that a unified organization would be more efficient and this served as a backdrop to the unification of January 1984 at Clichy in Paris. Indeed, one of the first discussion points at this meeting was the composition of the electoral list which was finally drawn up at a following meeting of the newly-created governing body of *Les Verts*, the CNIR, *(Conseil National Inter Régional)* at Montsouris (14 - 15 April 1984). The list was headed by a living anti-nuclear legend, Didier Anger who was suppported by Yves Cochet, S. Fernex and Jean Brière. At this time, A. Waechter was not among the leading figures. It was also noticeable that women were conspicuous by their absence with only 3 being present amongst the first 12 positions (S. Fernex, Ginette Skandrini, Andrée Buchmann).

It was also at this time that B. Lalonde distanced himself formally from the vertical axis of the environmental movement by resigning from the executive committee of the RAT and by announcing his intention to participate in the formation of an independent environmental list to fight the European elections (ERE: *Entente-Radicale-Ecologiste*) thereby severing all links with *Les Verts*. With hindsight, the first indications of such a move could perhaps be seen in the meagre 17 percent of votes that B. Lalonde received (in his absence) for first place on the European list at the aforementioned inaugural meeting of *Les Verts* in Clichy.

TABLE 1.10 European Elections 1984

	Votes Cast	*Les Verts*	Percent
Countrywide results	19,728,448	674,766	3.4

Source: Le Monde, 19 June 1984.

In the event, the results of these elections were relatively weak (see Table 1.10). By way of an explanation of, and justification for, the drop in the overall vote since the previous European elections of 1979, *Les Verts* themselves put forward three reasons. Firstly, the high percentage of abstentionists (43.3 percent); secondly, the (too) recent structural unification and thirdly, B. Lalonde's presence at the head of the rival ERE list which obtained 664,403 votes (3.4 percent). This presence was seen as a betrayal by the secretary of *Les Verts*, Michel Delore, who described it as a "knife thrust in the back" at the annual general meeting (AGM) of Dijon later that year.

These explanations apart, there was a question mark over the future given "the relative weakness of the environmental movement in France: far from the German 'Citizens initiatives' (300,000 to 400,000) and the alternative movement (600,000)."[53] On a more positive note, for the first time in French environmental history, the organization that went into the elections came out of them intact.

The AGM of the 2 - 3 November 1984 was the first of the unified organization and allowed observers to take its pulse. It was held in Dijon (Côtes d'Or) as a means of demonstrating the importance of regionalism within *Les Verts* and marked the beginning of a political strategy, led by the then leading spokespersons (Y. Cochet, D. Anger, J. Brière and Guy Marimot) of opening up *Les Verts* with a view to collaborating with other alternative political groups. G. Marimot, at one point, suggested that *Les Verts* had "one year to take off" and this strategy was reminiscent of that of *Les Amis de la Terre* during the 1970s whose aim was to link up with the oppositional social movements of that period (e.g. feminists, regionalists, consumers etc.). The most oft-cited political theme was that formulated by Y. Cochet when he suggested that *Les Verts* should be "radically reformist". That is, they should campaign for reforms which were "incompatible with the logic of productivism".[54] It was also noticeable that at this AGM, unemployment was voted as the main campaign for the following year as opposed to a strictly environmental theme.

Nineteen eighty-five was a testing time for *Les Verts*, both electorally and within their own activist circle. Electorally, it gave

TABLE 1.11 Cantonal Elections 1985

	Votes Cast	*Les Verts*	Percent
Countrywide results	11,473,755	90,735	0.8
Cantons with environmental candidates		90,735	4.8

Sources: *Le Monde*, 12 March 1985; Sainteny 1991: 78.

rise to the third environmental appearance in the cantonal elections (see Table 1.11). Despite the apparently low score, these results were in fact a sign of electoral progress. The cantonal elections are not considered to be an exercise in electoral mobilization (e.g. 34 percent abstention in 1985) and are, as we have seen, a difficult obstacle for a party without a long-standing local base. This notwithstanding, the environmentalists have increased their scores over the years. Between 1979 and 1982 the vote increased from 49,885 to 55,589 votes, even if the total percentage vote dropped slightly from 0.5 percent to 0.4 percent. However, in 1985, both the number of votes (90,735) and the total percentage vote (0.8 percent) rose. *Les Verts* themselves, while remaining conscious of the overall weak result considered this, nevertheless, to be the sign of an electoral base in the making (see *Lettre Contact* 2: 15 March 1985).

The French Secret Service versus Greenpeace. With regard to environmental activism, there were two tests for the recently formed *Verts*. The first was in the form of the sinking of the Greenpeace ship, *Rainbow Warrior*, by the French Secret Service in the port of Aukland on 10 July 1985. This act of 'State terrorism' was not over-exploited by *Les Verts* which was ostensibly surprising, but only ostensibly so. The *Rainbow Warrior* affair was, in reality, out of the environmentalists' reach even though the target was an environmental ship. This was because it was directly concerned with military policy[55] as Greenpeace was protesting against French nuclear testing in the south Pacific and the all-party consensus on the nuclear question has always been strong enough to stifle opposition. The newly-formed *Verts* were never in a position to exploit this act of international terrorism and indeed because of the latent public support for the action, somewhat fatalistically, they never really attempted to. At the same time, it must be said that access to the media on this subject was not easy.

The second test was an internal matter for *Les Verts* and concerned what became known as the 'Cochet affair'. In May, there were rumors that the Breton Y. Cochet, the leading spokesperson at that time, would stand as a candidate in the north of France at the legislative elections of 1986. The reason for this decision was that the constituency of the *Nord-Pas-de-Calais* was one of the marginal seats in which the environmentalists could hope to win a parliamentary seat.[56] Given the apparent lack of a suitable candidate, the local *Verts* asked Y. Cochet to head their list. Y. Cochet was willing to do this but certain important Breton activists were of a different opinion.

The conflict opposed, in reality, two conceptions of politics. The first was opportunist, in the noblest sense of the term; i.e. the opportunity of having a *député* (i.e. MP: Member of Parliament) was available and for a minority party such as *Les Verts* to let it pass by would be disastrous, was the analysis of those in favour. Those against considered that to present a candidate in a region other than his/her own was to practise politics in the same way as the major parties, so disliked. The conflict over this question was so acute that an internal Breton referendum was held to decide but on counting the votes, *Les Verts* were split down the middle. It was decided to leave the decision to the national governing body (CNIR) at their next meeting in Nantes (Loire-Atlantique, 28 September 1985), which supported the candidacy.

Two conclusions may be drawn from this episode. Firstly, this seemed anything but an alternative political practice. The fine distinctions which were made to justify the move (e.g. it was not 'parachuting' a candidate because *Les Verts* in the north asked Y. Cochet to stand) were, perhaps, less important than the perception of the maneuver by outsiders. Equally, there was major internal strife caused and the comment of one Breton activist during the aforementioned CNIR summed up this first lesson: "The problem is that we have not managed to practise politics in a different way" (R. Dantec, *Verts-Bretagne*).

The second conclusion concerns the distance between theory and practice concerning regionalism in environmental discourse. What was striking in this affair was the obvious surprise of the other regions represented at the CNIR of Nantes that such drama could be caused by this question. This seemed to indicate a contradiction between a discourse on decentralization clashing with a centralizing mentality. This second conclusion is corroborated by the fact that in supporting this electoral move, *Les Verts* gave precedence to the national elections over the regional ones which were to be held on the same day. As it transpired, the results of the legislative and regional elections destroyed all the nurtured illusions. The score in the legislative elections (see Table 1.12) was particularly weak when compared with the two previous campaigns and reflects the difficulties *Les Verts* had at this time in gaining recognition. In constituencies where environmentalists stood, for example, the score was down on both 1981 (3.3 percent) and 1978 (4.7 percent). The regional

TABLE 1.12 Legislative Elections 1986

	Votes Cast	*Les Verts*	Percent
Countrywide results	28,094,929	339,939	1.2
Constituencies with environmental candidates		339,939	2.7

Source: *Le Monde*, 18 March 1986.

TABLE 1.13 Regional Elections 1986

	Votes Cast	*Les Verts*	Percent
Countrywide results	27,381,866	643,474	2.4
Departments with environmental candidates		643,474	2.5

Source: *Le Monde*, 18 March 1986.

elections (see Table 1.13) brought a small ray of electoral sunshine in that three regional councillors were elected (D. Anger in Normandy; A. Waechter and A. Buchmann in Alsace).

The French Nuclear Information Services versus Chernobyl. Soon after these elections (26 April 1986), the nuclear accident which environmentalists had feared since the early 1970s happened in the USSR. On the 26 April 1986, the nuclear plant of Chernobyl sent out a cloud of radioactive dust across Europe. This event singled out France once again as official information channels led the public into believing that their country had been spared from the fallout. Two weeks after the event, however, Pierre Pellerin, head of the governmental information body on radioactive substances (SCPRI: *Service Central de Protection contre les Rayonnements Ionisants*) eventually admitted that the cloud had not been turned away at the French customs. *Les Verts* found themselves in the midst of a tragicomedy. They were criticized for not reacting sufficiently which led some to find 'reds' under the 'green bed'.

"We could have gloated but being right here is a bitter feeling" was the environmental reaction but, in reality, *Les Verts* were as impotent in this case as in that of the *Rainbow Warrior*. Ever since the Socialist Party had reconciled themselves with nuclear arms, the environmentalists were faced with a nuclear consensus that stretched from the Communist party to the Gaullist RPR (*Rassemblement pour la République*). Nuclear power (civil and military), it was heralded, was France's guarantee of independence and to be anti-nuclear was virtually synonymous with treason. Moreover, *Les Verts* were still smarting from their electoral rout. Given these circumstances, and coupled with traditional difficulties of access to the national medias, it was not surprising that little was heard from the French environmentalists as compared with the reaction in other European countries.

Red and Green, Seldom Seen

We have seen that the idea and practice of an 'alternative' society and economy were, and remain, features of environmentalism. Between 1985 and 1988, the political form that such an idea may take was a question of some importance for red and green activists.[57] In May 1985, *Les Verts* published a "call for a convergence of alternative and environmental forces" (*Appel à la convergence des forces alternatives et écologistes*). There had, in fact, been several attempts to create an alternative political movement but all were doomed without the participation of *Les Verts*. The most ambitious of these initiatives was undoubtedly that of the 'Rainbow' alliance (*Arc-en-Ciel*) in January 1987 which attempted to bring together:

> self-management activists, feminists, environmentalists, regionalists, third world activists (...) trade unions, neighborhood associations, anti-racist, non-violent and anti-nuclear movements.[58]

According to one of the texts amidst a wealth of literature, this was an attempt to found a movement of 'social environmentalism' (*écologie sociale*):[59]

> *Arc-en-Ciel* is trying to blend environmentalism and the 'social sector' (*le social*). In order to succeed, let's listen to each other without rushing, without fear and criticism and discover, step by step, what we have in common. Let us found in France, social environmentalism. It will take time, even if we have the example of the German Greens before us.[60]

The experience of Arc-en-Ciel is of interest for two reasons. Firstly, the 'social question' and the 'environmental question' are both supposed to be dealt with within *Les Verts*. That one of their then prominent spokespersons (i.e. P. Radanne) believed that they needed to come together elsewhere suggested otherwise. Secondly, the example of the German Greens (*Die Grünen*) is one that *Les Verts* have used when the circumstances fit; that is, the success of *Die Grünen* has been a permanent point of reference while their practices (red-green collaboration) are refused, hence the attempts principally by members of the alternative left to build this German-type social movement. The refusal of the vast majority of *Les Verts* to participate reflected this overwhelming desire to forge an autonomous political identity and culture which they felt would be impossible with ex-leftists who were seen as having lost all credibility:

> a certain social convergence, albeit conflictual, between *Les Verts* and alternative activists has often taken place (...) [but] (...) a mixture of struggles does not, simply by its diversity, create a social movement, especially if it is tainted by the practices of extreme-left organizations whose future, like it or not, seems in doubt. (*Appel à la convergence des forces alternatives et écologistes*)

The efforts of *Arc-en-Ciel* reached a watershed in 1987 as the presidential elections of the following year loomed; further proof that these elections structure the whole of French political life. On the 18 - 19 October 1987 it organized a conference in Lyon in which discussion centered on two related points. Firstly, the long-term question of political culture. The participants wished to draw the contours of a new political culture integrating alternative left and environmental theory. More significant, perhaps, was the desire to begin such a task from practices and social experimentation instead of ideology which reflected the desire to recapture the spirit of the 1970s innovatory effervescence lost under a Socialist government coming to terms with the enterprise culture. Secondly, the short-term question of the forthcoming presidential elections and the decision to support, or not, one of the two candidates closest to their concerns; i.e. the environmentalist A. Waechter or the dissident communist, Pierre Juquin. To help them decide, the two candidates in question spoke on the same platform for the first time during this conference. The eventual decision was that *Arc-en-Ciel* would not intervene in the presidential debate with a view to demonstrating that elections were less important than building a social movement.

The ambition of *Arc-en-Ciel* was not fulfilled as indeed it could not have been without the active support of *Les Verts* and it faded out in the run-up to the presidential elections of 1988 as the rivalry between the two candidates intensified.

The Waechter Era

Within *Les Verts*, 1986 was a turning point. At the November AGM, the foundations of the policy of total independence from other parties were laid down by A. Waechter. This was the beginning of a rift within *Les Verts* between those who wished to place the party at the heart of an alternative movement and those who refused such an idea. The new strategy incarnated by A. Waechter has been described as one directed more towards the defense of the natural environment than towards the social one. Certainly, the debate over the choice of campaigns for the following year indicated just this when A. De Swarte,[61] commenting on the choice of anti-racism as the main campaign for the next year, proclaimed: "We should have given priority to environmentalism. That's what we're famous for. We shouldn't have chosen anti-racism, it's too social." Such a vision of environmentalism was not to everyone's liking and a founder member of *Les Verts*, René Commandeur, reacted by shouting that "environmentalism is regressing!". Be that as it may have been, this AGM heralded a change in direction which was accompanied by a change of leadership. The previous spokespersons (Y. Cochet, D. Anger, J. Brière and G. Marimot) were all replaced and this was seen as a sanction for their (over)commitment to a political convergence with the alternative left. A. Waechter, a Doctor in Ecology, talked of "organic politics (...) when two organisms occupy the same place, one replaces the other"[62] and this is precisely what he did personally with regard to the dominant position held up until then by Y. Cochet and what the new spokespersons (A. Waechter, A. Buchmann, M. Delore, François Berthout) did with regard to the old. This cleavage reflected, and still does, two types of activists within *Les Verts* who have always had difficulty coexisting: those more involved in natural conservation and those whose political socialization has taken place in social struggle.

The size of Waechter's newfound majority was such (65.3 percent of the vote) that life was to become difficult for internal opposition. The first indication of this was the primaries for the environmental presidential candidature which A. Waechter easily won. The second was at the November AGM when Y. Cochet

TABLE 1.14 Presidential Elections 1988

	Votes Cast	Antoine Waechter	Percent
Countrywide results	30,282,950	1,145,502	3.8

Source: Le Monde, 26 April 1988.

persisted in his efforts to consider working with the left by presenting a motion (*Entrons en Politique*) which supported a contractual relationship with the PS; but such a suggestion remained heresy for most of those present. This AGM was in fact the launch pad for A. Waechter's presidential campaign and the heavy defeat of Y. Cochet's motion (14 percent) reflected this.

The campaign was not an easy one, financially speaking, on top of which the media seemed to have a distinct preference for the alternative left candidate, the well-known dissident communist Pierre Juquin. Despite this, the environmental score (see Table 1.14) was considered respectable as it almost equalled that of B. Lalonde in 1981 (i.e. 1,122,445 votes, 3.8 percent). These elections heralded the second mandate of F. Mitterrand whose first act in power was to call legislative elections. *Les Verts* were incapable of standing and decided to boycott what they termed as "TGV elections"[63] in which they stood no chance (despite this national position, certain environmentalists decided to stand; see Table 1.15).

The following September, and two months before the AGM, the cantonal elections offered another electoral test (see Table 1.16). The rate of abstention was extremely high (1st round: 50.9 percent, 2nd round: 52.5 percent) and *Les Verts* increased their previous score of 1985 with an average of 6.8 percent in the

TABLE 1.15 Legislative Elections 1988

	Votes Cast	Les Verts	Percent
Countrywide results	24,432,095	86,312	0.4

Source: Libération, 7 June 1988.

TABLE 1.16 Cantonal Elections 1988

	Votes Cast	Les Verts	Percent
Countrywide results:			
1st Round	9,117,156	151,069	1.7
2nd Round	5,973,240	6,966	0.1

Sources: *Le Monde*, 27 September 1988; *Le Monde*, 4 October 1988

Cantons in which they presented candidates (*Vert-Contact* N°80, 1988). None were elected but the progress in these difficult elections was confirmed.

The atmosphere of the AGM was electric. Many an appetite had been whetted by the presidential results and the raised expectations of the 'Waechterians' gave rise to some very unconvivial verbal exchanges. The new 'fundamentalists' made an appearance[64] and the electoral strategy was clearly stated: "we will never be efficient until we have overcome the electoral threshold of credibility."[65] In the votes on the motions, A. Waechter came out with an overall 66.6 percent majority, confirming the visible control he had on the party at this time. This control made it difficult for those alternative left activists who so desired to join *Les Verts* as entry was subject to intensive scrutiny. Pierre Juquin was the most famous victim of the fear that the greens would now be submerged by red entryism.[66]

The First Green Wave

Planet of the Year: Endangered Earth was how the magazine *Time* (2 January 1989) saw the 'green' year of 1989. The green wave began to sweep over France in March at the municipal elections which produced surprisingly high scores (see Table 1.17). The depth of these results becomes clearer when the environmental scores in towns of over 30,000 inhabitants are considered (see Table 1.18).

These scores were well above the national average and reinforce analyses on the urban nature of the environmental vote.[67] It was also noticeable that in 12 of the 16 towns the scores increased, which was seen as a vindication of the traditional strategy of refusing to stand down for other candidates.

TABLE 1.17 Municipal Elections 1989

Countrywide Results

	Votes Cast	*Les Verts*	Percent
1st Round	26,186,678	353,416	1.5[a]
2nd Round	11,859,830	112,864	0.9

[a] Percentage does not tally because of different voting system in *communes* of less than 3,500 inhabitants (*panachage*). See *Le Monde*, 15 March 1989.

Sources: *Le Monde*, 15 March 1989; *Le Monde*, 23 March 1989; Sainteny 1991: 78.

TABLE 1.18 Municipal Elections 1989

Results in Towns of over 30,000 Inhabitants

Department	Town	1st Round *Verts* Percent	2nd Round *Verts* Percent
22	Saint-Brieuc	14.6	22.2
25	Besançon	12.9	14
29	Quimper	14.5	13.5
49	Cholet	13.5	19.4
56	Vannes	13.6	21.3
56	Lorient	15.1	20.4
67	Strasbourg	12.8	8.9
68	Colmar	14.1	24.2
68	Mulhouse	12.6	9.6
69	Caluire	13.8	19.1
69	Saint-Priest	10.8	10.6
75	Paris XIV	10.6	17.1
82	Montauban	10.9	16.1
86	Poitiers	11	12.5
87	Limoges	11.1	19.5
92	Nanterre	10.5	12.6

Source: *Le Monde* 15 March 1989

TABLE 1.19 European Elections 1989

	Votes Cast	*Les Verts*	Percent
Countrywide results	18,112,155	1,919,797	10.6

Sources: *Le Monde*, 20 June 1989; *Ouest France*, 20 June 1989

Les Verts won 1,369 municipal seats which was not as many as the 3,000 that A. Waechter had aimed for but which, nevertheless, was an increase of 45 percent on the 1983 municipal elections.[68] In Rennes (Ille et Vilaine), the environmentalists kept a sufficiently clear head by thanking their electors but also "the Breton rivers, the ozone layer and the Amazonian forest which were a great help."[69] They and most people were aware that environmentalism was in fashion[70] even if several years of constant activism had paved the way.

Given this favorable context, the European elections came at the right time (see Table 1.19). On the 18 June 1989, nine environmentalists, two of whom were 'invited' (*candidats d'ouverture*),[71] were elected, giving them the largest environmental group in the European Parliament.

The Return of Brice Lalonde's Comet: 1988 - 1992

Brice Lalonde came back onto the environmental stage in 1988. Two days before the presidential elections, he published an article in *Le Monde* entitled *Pour l'Environnement* in which he expressed doubts about the need for an environmental candidate or party, and in which he came out in support of the socialist candidate F. Mitterrand. Three weeks later he became State Secretary for the Environment in the new government. Four years after their 'divorce' at Clichy, the rivalry between the ex-champion of environmentalism (Lalonde) and *Les Verts* had begun again. Some observers suspected that inviting Lalonde into the socialist government was a political maneuver by the Socialist Party to weaken the rising electoral threat of the environmentalists but whatever the motivations environmentalism was off to a new, divided start.

Initially, the return of B. Lalonde did not seem to worry *Les Verts* too much and both sides went about their respective businesses. *Les Verts* renewed their confidence in A. Waechter during an unusually uneventful AGM in Marseilles (November 1989)[72] and B. Lalonde went to work both nationally and internationally (see below). However, this period of feigning ignorance came to a somewhat abrupt end when B. Lalonde decided that he needed an organization to support his governmental activity. So it was, that on the 11 May 1990, with the support of 150 MPs from different parties (e.g. Jean-Louis Borloo and Haroun Tazieff [independent], Jean-Michel Belorgey [PS], Alain Carignon [RPR]) he created *Génération Ecologie*. From the outset, the political target of *Génération Ecologie* was clear when B. Lalonde defined himself as an "active environmentalist" who was confronted with "fundamentalists" (i.e. *Les Verts*) whom he labeled "sectarian" (*Ouest France*: 12 May 1990). *Les Verts* replied by stating that *Génération Ecologie* was simply an offshoot of *Génération Mitterrand* (*Vert-Contact* N° 155, 1990).

There are two interesting aspects to B. Lalonde's initiative. Firstly, his organization is not a political party since *Génération Ecologie* aims to be the "matrix of a movement of ambitious ideas and actions". In this, Lalonde has retained the broad based strategy of *Les Amis de la Terre* of the 1970s by demonstrating his distaste for established parties and their internal discipline. Secondly, the struggle for the environmental electoral 'treasure' has begun with the advent of *Génération Ecologie*. Proof is no longer needed that it exists and whether it is made up of ex-socialist voters (D.D.S: *Déçus du Socialisme*[73]) or confirmed environmentalists matters little. Moreover, B. Lalonde realized at this time that he had to launch his movement while in office. As for the strategy, it was a mixture of spontaneity and tactics.

Tactically, B. Lalonde exploited the divisions within *Les Verts* and contradicted Waechter whenever he could. When Waechter was portrayed as being more interested in the natural environment, Lalonde would state that "society had to be re-socialized." When Waechter refused to negotiate with other parties before having a written contract, Lalonde suggested that it was necessary to "accept alliances." When Waechter claimed that "our ambition is, first of all to create a cultural majority in this country which can lean on a political majority",[74] Lalonde replied that the best way forward was to environmentalize politics rather than politicizing environmentalism. But his best move was to make an offer which *Les Verts* could not refuse.

In October 1990, he successively offered the Presidency of the new Environment Agency (AEME: *Agence pour l'Environnement et pour la Maîtrise de l'Energie*)[75] to two prominent members of *Les Verts* (Y. Cochet and Christian Brodhag). Y. Cochet was the first to be contacted and refused the offer. Christian Brodhag did the same but then Y. Cochet reconsidered the proposition and put it to a vote within *Les Verts*. This was enough to create total confusion, with some for and some against. B. Lalonde himself put an end to their dilemma by withdrawing his offer, officially due to the stances of *Les Verts* on the Gulf War and on the National Front, but also because of the 'Brière affair' (see below).

The position with regard to the French National Front (extreme-right wing) was the big question for *Les Verts* in 1990.[76] Quite obviously, the political culture of the *Les Verts* is light years away from the National Front for any commentator with the slightest notion of French politics. However, *Les Verts* are particularly good at scoring own goals, as they did in voting a motion at their AGM in Strasbourg (Alsace, November 1990) which read that, "forming alliances against Le Pen is admitting that what we are opposed to in other political forces is less important than what opposes us to Le Pen".[77] The desire, at times obsessive, to maintain political autonomy by being 'neither left nor right' produced this remark. The least that can be said is that many a prospective elector was left dubious as to the real position of certain environmentalists on the issue of the National Front. This kind of doubt could only be to B. Lalonde's benefit and so it was that he was voted "the best spokesperson" for environmentalism (40 percent) ahead of A. Waechter (22 percent) in December (*Le Monde*, 16 - 17 December 1990).

The other half of B. Lalonde's strategy to conquer the environmental electorate was more spontaneous in that he took full advantage of two events: the Gulf War and the 'Brière affair'. The Gulf War produced a real opposition between *Génération*

Ecologie and *Les Verts* on the question of political non-violence. For B. Lalonde, it was "not a good thing for environmentalism to be identified with pacifism"[78] (*Le Monde*, 26 January 1991) whereas *Les Verts*, refused "this war and [called] on all those people who are concerned for our future on this planet to speak out against the use of this war to control oil resources and stimulate the arms trade" (*Vert-Contact* 185, 1991).

In reality, even though the party line was against the war, *Les Verts* were divided on this issue. The majority were against the 'Desert Storm' operation either on principles of pacifism ("Whether B. Lalonde likes it or not, environmentalism and war are and will remain incompatible" − *Vert-Contact* 185, 1991) or because they believed the embargo to be sufficient, and a minority were in favour.

During the debate on the Gulf War, the 'Brière affair' shook the foundations of *Les Verts* and supplied B. Lalonde with extra ammunition. This affair began when J. Brière produced a text entitled "The belligerent role of Israel and the Zionist lobby" at the CNIR of the 6 April 1991. The text was considered anti-semitic by many activists and when the press was given a copy, Brière's days as a member of *Les Verts* were numbered, despite his status as a founder member of the party. By the end of the year, he was excluded but the political damage had been done. Despite several condemnations of the text and of the National Front, public doubts over the 'nature' of environmentalism had been widely voiced and *Les Verts* became easy prey for experienced politicians wishing to clad them in black shirts.

It was amidst this atmosphere of suspicion as to the real intentions of environmentalism that *Les Verts* held their AGM of 1991 in St Brieuc (Côtes d'Armor, Brittany), four months before what looked like very promising regional elections for both environmental camps. This Breton AGM, at which everyone put on electoral smiles, produced nevertheless a clash over the question of how to react to the National Front in the future regional councils. The Breton, Y. Cochet, suggested that *Les Verts* should "not participate in the running of any region with any party that shared power with the National Front in another region." This was rejected and A. Waechter came out unscathed by proposing that *Les Verts* should be flexible in the future regional councils with a view to "maintaining the credibility of the proportional electoral system and to not block the institutions."

The Regional and Cantonal Elections of 1992

The Regional Elections. These were to be the first elections since 1984 in which *Les Verts* did not have the monopoly on environmentalism. As they approached, the competition between the environmental rivals intensified, given that they could no longer ignore each other. *Les Verts* maintained that the real environmentalists were in their party but that did not make much difference to the voting intentions or the results (see Table 1.20).

France is divided into 22 regions and the elections were held under a system of departmental lists, which in itself was a paradox. That is to say, each department within a region had several lists from which to choose and candidates were elected directly from these to the regional council. A more detailed study of the results shows that the race between the environmentalists ended in a virtual dead-heat (see Table 1.21).

The overall results were surprisingly similar. The environmental vote was much more widely spread over the country than for the European elections of 1989 and this was due, no doubt to the presence of B. Lalonde's party. Equally striking was the high score of the latter in *Ile de France* (22 seats). *Ile de France* includes 8 departments, one of which is Paris in which *Génération Ecologie* took 5 seats, as opposed to *Les Verts'* 2 seats. This was an example of a more urban vote for Lalonde's party and a more rural vote for *Les Verts*. Where there was a straight

TABLE 1.20 Regional Elections 1992

	Votes Cast	Environmentalists	Percent
Countrywide results:	24,431,676	*Verts*: 1,659,798	6.8
		GE: 1,744,350	7.1

Source: Libération, 24 March 1992.

TABLE 1.21 Environmental Results in the Regional Elections by Region and by Party 1992

	Verts		Génération Ecologie	
	Percent	Seats	Percent	Seats
Alsace	12.6	(6)	6.7	(3)
Aquitaine	4.7	(2)	8.1	(7)
Auvergne	7.4	(3)	4.3	(2)
Basse-Normandie	7.5	(4)	7.9	(4)
Bourgogne	7.5	(5)	3.5	(2)
Bretagne	6.8	(6)	8.7	(6)
Centre	6.3	(3)	7	(5)
Champagne Ardennes	7	(2)	5.9	(2)
Corse			5	(0)
Franche Comté	8.4	(3)	7.6	(2)
Haute-Normandie	7.6	(4)	7.1	(4)
Ile de France	7.7	(15)	10.7	(22)
Languedoc-Rousillon	5.5	(3)	7.3	(4)
Limousin	7	(2)	3.1	(1)
Lorraine	8.7	(5)	8.3	(6)
Midi Pyrénées	7.9	(6)	1.1	(1)[a]
Nord-Pas-de-Calais	6.4	(8)	5.7	(6)
Pays de Loire	6.9	(6)	8.1	(7)
Picardie	8.1	(5)	7.4	(4)
Poitou Charentes	8.1	(4)	6.6	(3)
Provence-Alpes-Côtes d'Azur (PACA)	4.5	(3)	3.5	(3)
Rhône Alpes	7	(10)	8.6	(11)
TOTAL		(105)		(105)

[a] There were joint lists between Génération Ecologie and Les Verts in 3 of the 8 departments of this region.

Sources: Le Monde, 24 March 1992; Libération 24 March 1992; Vert-Contact N°239 1992.

TABLE 1.22 Cantonal Elections 1992

1st Round	Votes Cast	Environmentalists	Percent
Countrywide results:	10,276,873	Verts: 815,454	7.9
		GE: 179,448	1.7
Cantons with		Verts: 815,454	11.1
environmental candidates:		GE: 179,448	11.3
2nd Round			
Countrywide results:	8,540,173	Verts:143,432	1.7
,		GE: 40,142	0.5

Sources: Libération, 24 March 1992; Le Monde, 31 March 1992

run-off between the two parties, B. Lalonde's did better. In the 77 departments (out of 96) in which this happened, Les Verts were ahead of Lalonde's party in 28 whereas Génération Ecologie was ahead in the other 49.

The Cantonal Elections. Les Verts have been present at these elections since 1985 although, as we have seen, non-aligned environmental candidates have stood since 1979. In these 1992 elections, they put up 1,400 candidates in the first round. In the second, they had 70 left, one of whom actually won a seat (Jean Baudoin Prahecq, Deux Sèvres) which was considered to be a feat. Not surprisingly, Génération Ecologie did not present many candidates for their first attempt (see Table 1.22).

Reactions. The first reaction to the overall environmental results was one of general satisfaction concerning the progress of electoral environmentalism with a total of 14.7 percent of the vote (Les Verts + Génération Ecologie + independent environmentalists). The second was a mixture of moderate disappointment and delight, depending on which side of the fence one was on. Les Verts were certainly not elated by their own score at the regional elections. It was a threefold rise on their score of 1986 (2.4 percent) when only they were present, but down from the heights reached during the European elections of 1989 (10.6 percent).

Many of *Les Verts*, such as Jean Louis Vidal, Parisian municipal councillor and director of *Les Verts'* campaign, considered the result "unfair", given the work they had done over the years. But since when is politics fair? *Les Verts* seemed to accept that their image needed changing if they were to reach wider sections of the population. The question is, of course, how far can a party change without losing its soul?

Génération Ecologie was delighted with rivalling the score of the 'official' environmentalists. For an organization created only 20 months previously (May 1990), this success would seem to be further confirmation of an important feature of French political culture: out of the State, out of the public mind. The importance of having a Minister for the Environment at the head of an electoral organization is, in itself, sizeable. In an industrial society beginning to take stock of environmental problems, this position took on even more weight and the media attention reinforced this. This was, of course, *Les Verts'* analysis and within the context of communication strategy (of increasing importance in Western elections) there is no doubt that B. Lalonde floored A. Waechter and his party. The former easily managed to exploit the latter's apparent sectarianism in refusing to join environmental forces. *Les Verts* did not consider the recently-recruited members of *Génération Ecologie* to be real environmentalists at all, especially given that a large proportion had recently left the Socialist Party. Lalonde's answer to that was that he had always wished to work with people from across the political spectrum.

Whatever the analysis, these results show what can be achieved in a very short time in modern politics. Environmentalism is no longer the sole property of *Les Verts* and this is a reality with which they now have to come to terms.

The week following these elections, B. Lalonde left the government. After fours years of "getting his hands dirty" he wanted to "go back to the rank and file". He (and all those who helped him) had managed, nevertheless, to get certain things done during his spell in power. On the international scene he had contributed to the ratification of the Montreal Protocol on the reduction of CFC gases (1988), the European agreement on car pollution, the international summit of the Hague on atmospheric protection (March 1989), the regulation of international trade in waste (Bâle, March 1989), the embargo on imports of ivory and the attempts to transform the Antarctic into an area of natural conservation.

Nationally speaking, B. Lalonde's most important contribution was, perhaps, the submission of his 'Green Plan' (*Plan Vert*) in June 1990. This included the creation of the aforementioned Agency for the Environment with several local antennae (DIREN: *Directions Régionales de l'Environnement*) and that of an 'Institute for the Environment' to be used as a form of environmental data base. In January 1992, he presented another important measure in the form of a new 'Law on Water' which replaced the existing law of 1962. Apart from the necessity for such a revamp, the novelty of this law was the extensive consultation of environmental associations prior to its final version. This made a change from the traditional technocratic presentation of governmental projects. Despite the pitifully low budget (1980: 0.111 percent of the State budget, 1990: 0.063 percent) B. Lalonde managed to further the idea that all ministerial decisions had environmental consequences. Outside of government, his opposition to major projects such as the road tunnel of Somport[79] and the water barrages on the Loire river (*Le Monde*, 10 August 1991) gave succour to the demonstrators.

In reality, however, B. Lalonde left the government because of his criticism of the Socialist Party's attempts to lay claim to his work in office. Environmentalism was, and remains, in fashion in France and Lalonde's presence in government was considered by the Socialists to be their trump-card and proof of their environmental credentials. Lalonde was of a different opinion, as he had to be if he wished *Génération Ecologie* to retain any electoral credibility. He left, therefore, in a huff of indignation but with his organization intact, 100 regional counsellors and the prospect of sharing an electoral cake with *Les Verts* in the legislative elections of March 1993. *Les Verts* were contacted to form a new government but they refused, not wishing to bale the Socialists out one year before the decisive legislative elections. On the other hand, they managed a real political scoop when Marie-Christine Blandin was elected president of the regional council in the north of France (*Nord-Pas-de-Calais*) with the support of the local Socialists. This was an event worthy of note as she was the first woman to reach such a position and, also, the first environmentalist.

The two environmental camps came out of these elections in different frames of mind; *Génération Ecologie* was euphoric and *Les Verts* were dubious. Dubious as to the state of environmentalism and of their future in that their eight-year-old existence had given them no advantage over the two-year-old (media) existence of *Génération Ecologie*. How likely were they to create the aspired to "cultural majority" (A. Waechter) in such conditions? And what were the prospects in the legislative elections of 1993 under a difficult electoral system for minority parties if there were two rival organizations?

With these questions in mind, *Les Verts* went into summer recess to finish organizing the *Assises de l'Ecologie*, the aim of which was to rebuild the bridges with civil society which had been weakened along the electoral trek of the 1980s.[80] In the final forum of this meeting, the presence of B. Lalonde (among others) was sufficient to set tongues wagging as to an eventual electoral alliance for 1993 which, sure enough, came about with a protocol agreement on the 3 November 1992. This agreement between *Les Verts* and *Génération Ecologie* held that there would be a single environmental candidate in each constituency (*circonscription*) for the legislative elections of March 1993. It was a protocol agreement because the members of the two respective organizations had to ratify it at separate meetings during the weekend of the 14 - 15 November 1992. *Génération Ecologie* did it by clapping whereas *Les Verts* took a vote (70.7 percent in favour).

The *Entente Ecologiste* and the French Legislative Elections of March 1993

The agreement between the two environmental camps was called the *Entente Ecologiste* and it gave them a head start in the campaign even if the foundations for such a pact were perhaps not as solid as they might have been, following the vote on

Maastricht.[81] B. Lalonde thought the *Entente Ecologiste* was "magnificent" although A. Waechter simply saw it as electoral agreement designed to overcome the "obstacles" of the voting system. This typically low key reaction was also a reflection of the difficulty he and others had experienced in obtaining the approval of activists for such an agreement at the AGM of *Les Verts* in November 1992 (Chambéry, Savoie). But agreement there was, and the environmental 'Entente cordiale' soon found itself attempting to explain the reasoning behind a 'neither right nor left' philosophy of politics to a bemused public opinion weaned on 25 years of Gaullist Republican political divides.

The institutional right-wing made a few attempts to woo the environmentalists but did not overstate its case, having no real need for anybody's help. Nicolas Sarkozy, RPR and future spokesperson for the incoming government, suggested that "in a second round run-off between a socialist and an environmentalist, we would support the latter" (*Ouest France*, 3 February 1993). Charles Millon, UDF, hoped for a government "which went beyond 50 percent, bringing together the RPR, the UDF and the new movements such as the environmentalists" (*Ouest France*, 3 February 1993). Gérard Longuet, president of the *Parti Républicain*, considered that the example given by environmentalists in the regional councils was a precedent: "Since the regions have been a testing ground and have shown that it is possible to work together without mutual destruction, why can't we try it out at a national level?" (*Libération*, 5 February 1993). However, these conciliatory remarks came to little when the RPR-UDF programme was published. Dominique Voynet, spokesperson for *Les Verts*, immediately qualified it as "frightening" and couldn't see herself in a government inspired by it. The relations between the PS and the *Entente Ecologiste* were, however, a totally different affair, given that two-thirds of environmental voters are ex-PS voters.

The PS worked up to these crucial elections with the enthusiasm of a prisoner on death row. For weeks, opposition pundits and the media had been claiming that the end was nigh with predictions of an electoral rout for the party in power and, indeed, it was not in the best of health. The contaminated blood

TABLE 1.23 Voting Intentions for the Legislative Elections 1993

| | BVA | | CSA | |
	PS	Environmentalists	PS	Environmentalists
January	19.5	19	17.5	19
February	20	17	17.5	19.5

Sources: BVA surveys: (1) 15 - 20 January 1993; survey of 2,033 people over the age of 18 (*Libération*, 28 January 1993); (2) 1 - 4 February 1993; survey of 2,019 people over the age of 18 (*Le Monde*, 12 February 1993). CSA surveys: (1) 18 - 19 January 1993; survey of 808 people over the age of 18 (*Libération*, 28 January 1993); (2) 8 - 9 February 1993; survey of 1,006 people over the age of 18 (*Le Monde*, 12 February 1993).

affair, in which several people contracted AIDS through blood transfusions, and a series of other politico-financial scandals had seriously damaged its credibility over the preceeding few years. To take but one political example, the famous Rennes Congress of March 1990 had shown the party oligarchy to be far more interested in faction struggles than social change. This highly mediatized Congress had surprised and shocked many a socialist sympathizer.

Whatever the reasons for the disappointment with the PS, the winds of change were certainly evident in the voting intentions (see Table 1.23[82]). The environmentalists had been trying to woo the D.D.S. (*Déçus Du Socialisme*) for the previous ten years. Now, at last, it seemed a real possibility that massive numbers of them would finally take a leap into the environmental unknown. At the PS headquarters however, these figures set bells ringing and red lights flashing. The irrelevant environmentalists had become extremely relevant, electorally at least. What should be done?

The 'Big Bang'. It was Michel Rocard who came up with an answer, if not *the* answer; the political 'big bang'. Rocard has for some time been considered as the natural socialist candidate for the 1995 presidential elections and the Fifth French Republic is so structured that this election is the pinnacle of institutional political activity in the country. On the 17 February, he decided to abandon his Gaullian-like stance and take an active part in the campaign, realizing that he was likely to suffer from the potential political fallout of an expected electoral disaster. What he proposed was the creation of a new eco-socialist movement, even if he didn't call it that.

> What we need is a vast, open and modern movement, outward looking and rich in its diversity. A movement bringing together all those who share the same values of solidarity and social change. This movement would include reformist environmentalists, centrists from the social tradition, communist renovators and human rights activists. (M. Rocard: *Le Monde*, 19 February 1993)

This new movement, quite obviously, implied the eventual demise of the PS, the party created by F. Mitterrand. Hence the reticence of certain prominent Socialists, not least of whom, Laurent Fabius, still head of the PS at this time.[83]

Rocard is one of the few socialists who sees further than the next elections. Coming from the alternative left (ex-PSU), he understands that environmentalism in some form will be around for some time and would rather work with it than against it. Having taken this first initiative, he followed it up with a second by pushing the PS into taking a unilateral position for the second round run-offs; i.e. they promised before the first round to stand down for any candidate in the "progressive camp" (*camp de progrès*) and included the environmentalists in this definition. This was a very astute move as it avoided beforehand any embarrassing negotiations during the two rounds and, secondly, it placed the environmentalists on the left whether they liked it or not. In doing this the PS was going beyond the PC for electoral support and weakening the traditional '*Front Commun*' (PS/PC) strategy of the left.

These two initiatives, however, were not enough to change the face of the results (see Table 1.24). The environmentalists are fairly used to electoral hangovers, but this one was particularly painful given the final opinion poll forecasts.[84] On a positive note, they had increased their first round score considerably from the last legislative outing in 1988 (0.4 percent). They had also managed to force a debate on work sharing which had become a major theme in the final phase of the campaign. But, at the end of the day, they had not managed to enter Parliament. Several reasons may be put forward.

TABLE 1.24 Legislative Elections 1993

1st Round	Votes Cast	Entente Ecologiste	Percent
Countrywide results:	25,442,403	Verts: 1,022,749	4.1
		GE: 921,925	3.6
2nd Round [a]			
Countrywide results:	20,632,930	Verts: 20,088	0.1
		GE: 17,403	0.1

[a] The two remaining environmental hopes of the second round (Dominique Voynet of Les Verts and Christine Barthet of Génération Ecologie) were both beaten. The right-wing coalition (UPF) won a crushing 448 parliamentary seats from a total of 577. The left-wing coalition (PS/MRG) won 67. The remaining seats went to: PC: 25, Other right-wing: 36, Others: 1. No Front National candidates were elected.

Sources: Le Monde, 23 March 1993; Le Monde, 30 March 1993.

Firstly, it appears clear that outside issues concerning nature, the environmentalists' credibility remains weak. This has been a constant problem for them and their attempts during the campaign to shift the debate onto social grounds were apparently unconvincing. In a poll carried out between the two rounds, 43 percent still saw them as conservation specialists. Secondly, the strategy of the Entente Ecologiste in general and the political zigzagging of B. Lalonde in particular was heavily criticized. There did not seem to be any political direction to the environmental campaign. The four spokespersons of Les Verts and B. Lalonde for Génération Ecologie went off in their own directions. Moreover, their attempts at attracting media attention and their discourse once they had done so did little to support their wish to practise politics in a different way: "By trying to speak like the others, they became inaudible" (Libération, 23 March 1993). B. Lalonde was true to form; a complete political maverick who confused not only electors but seasoned politicians as well: "I don't know what B. Lalonde's position is. I don't have time to listen to the radio every hour" (L. Fabius). Time will tell whether the Entente Ecologiste between Les Verts and Génération Ecologie will survive but an overwhelming impression after the event was summed up by J. L. Saux in Le Monde (23 March 1993):

"Perhaps they wouldn't have done any better divided but at least the respective images of the two organizations wouldn't be so blurred".

The third reason concerns the environmental electorate which remains extremely fragile, not to say volatile. Polls illustrated this impression of instability and an analysis of the vote itself underlines it. In a poll on voting intentions carried out by BVA in February (1 - 4), 46 percent of potential environmental voters replied that they could yet change their minds, a figure well above the average of 33 percent. On the day, 39 percent of votes came from people who had made up their mind in the three or four days before the elections and only half of those who had voted for the environmentalists at the previous year's regional elections did so at these legislative ones. When both organizations stood independently at the regional elections last year, they gained 14 percent of the vote. In joining forces, they scored half that much albeit in a different type of election. The electoral bet was that 2 X 7 percent = 14 percent when forces are joined. It did not in these elections and when all is said and done perhaps this indicates that their respective electorates, however volatile, are quite simply different.[85] Both are centered on intellectuals (e.g. teachers, medical professions) but that of *Génération Ecologie* is more upper middle class than that of *Les Verts. Génération Ecologie* is also perceived as more moderate than *Les Verts.*

Moreover, it became clear that the structure of the environmental vote had changed since the regional elections of the previous year. The environmentalists may have retained a large part of their traditional supporters (e.g. young people, women) but they have lost their potential electorate (e.g. certain sections of the working class, D.D.S., people less interested in politics) which had voted for them, somewhat surprisingly it must be said, in 1992.

Some say that this electorate is also easily fooled given that around 3 percent of votes went to a succession of pseudo-environmental lists (e.g. *Génération Verte, Nouveaux Ecologistes, Ecologistes Indépendants*). These false environmental lists were used by B. Lalonde (but not Waechter) as the explanation for the weak score but of course, as we can see, this is not a sufficient explanation.

The fourth reason concerns the socialists. In the run up to these elections, the environmentalists had become the thorn in their foot. Never quite sure how to react towards them, many socialists adopted a harder line once the polls took a turn for the worse. Criticism of the environmentalists' 'neither right nor left' stance became louder ("The French people have a right to know who the environmentalists would govern with": Pierre Bérégovoy, 30 January 1993) with one national leader (G. Fuchs) going so far as to suggest that "An environmental vote is a wasted vote" (18 February 1993). However, one socialist, Michel Rocard, had his own strategy. Once the electoral dust had settled, it became clear that his 'big bang' had stolen the initiative from the *Entente Ecologiste*. The subsequent political fall-out remains to be seen but the effect on the campaign was decisive.

From December to February, the environmentalists had taken the lead in political communication and they were courted left, right and center. Lip service was paid by all and sundry to their ideas on work sharing (*Front National* apart) and each party wanted an *'écolo'* on its platform. However, once the heavy electoral machines went into gear, the PS in particular, they struggled to keep up. The 'big bang' brought them down to earth with a bump, as was painfully illustrated by their inability to react in any coherent political manner to it. The final 'kiss of death' was delivered when the PS, pushed by Rocard, declared that it would unilaterally stand down for environmental candidates in any second round run off favorable to them.

The 'big bang' may not have made any difference to the overall socialist disaster but it has modified the future situation between the PS and environmentalists. The former, now led by Rocard, has begun a serious attempt to bring the latter under its wing. The presidential elections take place in 1995 and Rocard hopes to be there. The scene is set for an ideological battle over the environmental label and within a political landscape now dominated by the right, the slogan 'neither right nor left' may have trouble surviving.

As for relations between *Les Verts* and *Génération Ecologie*, opinions are divided. The *Entente Ecologiste* was only designed for these elections, which in itself did not lend too much credibility to it for the prospective voter. Noël Mamère (*Génération Ecologie*) is of the opinion that its survival is synonymous with that of environmentalism in France whereas Dominique Voynet believes that it needs more substance (*contenu*). One proposition put forward by Gérard Onesta (*Les Verts*) brings back memories of their creation in 1984; i.e. to form a new organization called *Les Ecologistes* with two sub-headings: *Les Verts-Génération Ecologie*.[86] In 1984, B. Lalonde was not interested in working with *Les Verts*. Would he be more interested this time around?

Conclusion. Environmentalism celebrated its twentieth birthday in 1993[87] and it has come a long way since the first activists branded the anarchist slogan "elections are a fool's game!".

There are three acts to this environmental drama; one for each decade. Act one covers the 1970s. This was a decade in which the horizontal axis of environmentalism was strongest and when there was a strong articulation between the environmentalists and other social movements (e.g. regionalists, third world activists, alternative left etc.). It was a decade in which bridges existed between the environmentalists and the institutional opposition (e.g. PS, CFDT) and during which the former divided their time between political and civil society by participating actively in a vast movement of social and political transformation. This period ended with the election of F. Mitterrand in May 1981 as many of the best elements of civil society (e.g. prominent activists of trade unions, associations) were sucked into the governmental machine. The aforementioned social movements fell apart and at the beginning of the 1980s, the environmentalists began their walk into a political 'Wasteland'.

Act two began with the first steps into the 'Wasteland'. The immediate aftermath of the presidential elections and the decision by the Socialist government to pursue the nuclear programme convinced the remaining few environmentalists who had retained any socialist illusions that there was still work to be done. Of those who stayed, and many did not, the conflict was such that unification seemed a long way off. When it came in 1984, the investment in organizational work and electioneering was such that the vertical axis took over from the horizontal one. B. Lalonde went his own way and within *Les Verts*, a real political battle began between the 'social' and 'natural' bows of the environmental vessel; a battle which only really abated for the space of a war (in the Gulf). Outside of *Les Verts*, the attempts to create a red-green alliance appear, in retrospect, as the final throes of the 'class of May 1968'.

The end of the 'Wasteland' came into sight when A. Waechter made an honorable showing at the presidential elections of 1988, underlining the importance of this type of election in French politics. It coincided (or was stimulated by) a world-wide interest in, and realization of, environmental degradation. At the municipal and European elections of 1989, the line of natural environmentalism and strict political autonomy seemed to have won out. Four years of hard work in carving out an organization based on internal democracy and decentralization seemed to have paid dividends. *Les Verts* were ready to take on the 'big guns' but had lost their foothold in civil society. Then the 'big bad wolf' (B. Lalonde) reappeared and the third act began. Environmentalism is no longer the property of *Les Verts* and since the legislative elections of 1993, they and *Génération Ecologie* have now to operate under a right-wing government. How this will modify the already sizeable task of ecologizing politics and society remains to be seen.

In the following chapter, we will analyze the political culture of the environmentalists. This represents an important factor in any social movement and one which will help us to unravel the environmental web.

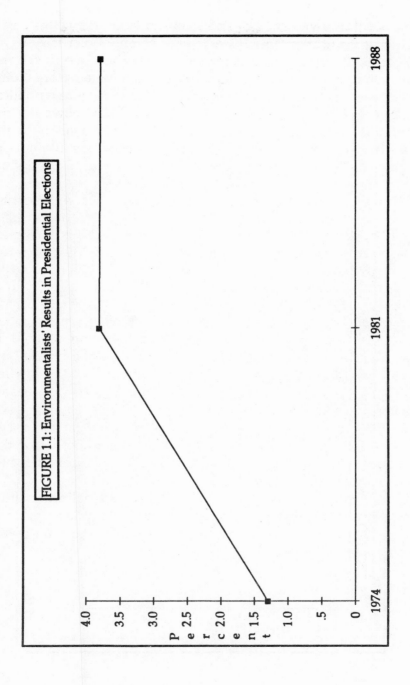

FIGURE 1.1: Environmentalists' Results in Presidential Elections

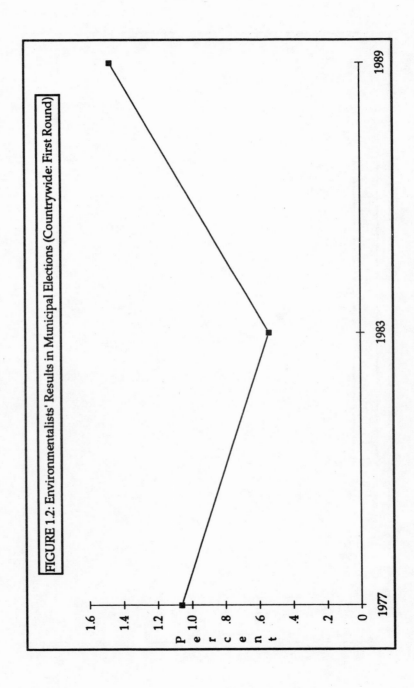

FIGURE 1.2: Environmentalists' Results in Municipal Elections (Countrywide: First Round)

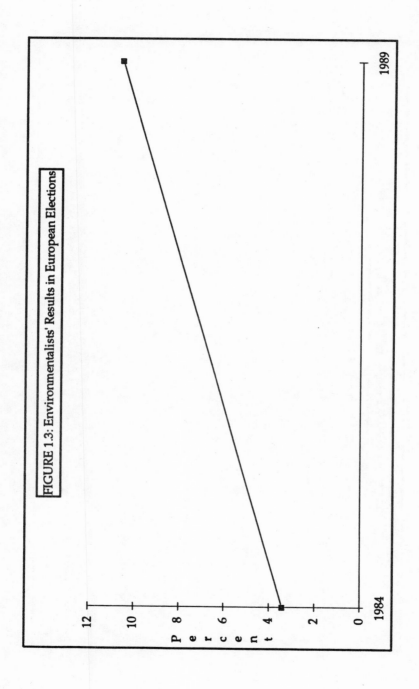

FIGURE 1.3: Environmentalists' Results in European Elections

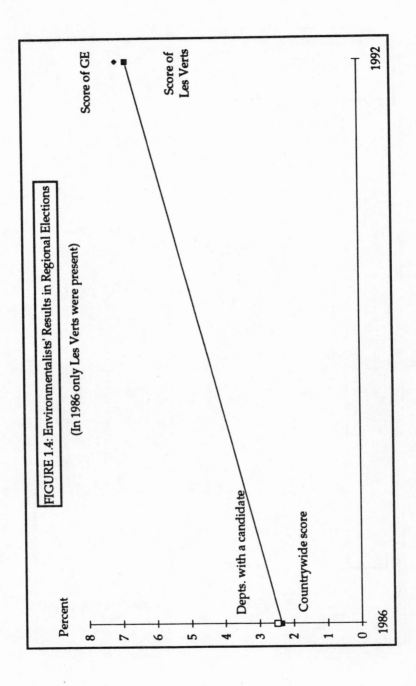

FIGURE 1.4: Environmentalists' Results in Regional Elections

(In 1986 only Les Verts were present)

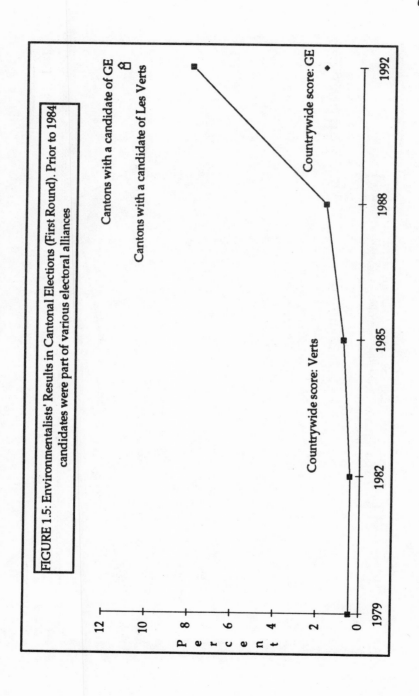

FIGURE 1.5: Environmentalists' Results in Cantonal Elections (First Round). Prior to 1984 candidates were part of various electoral alliances

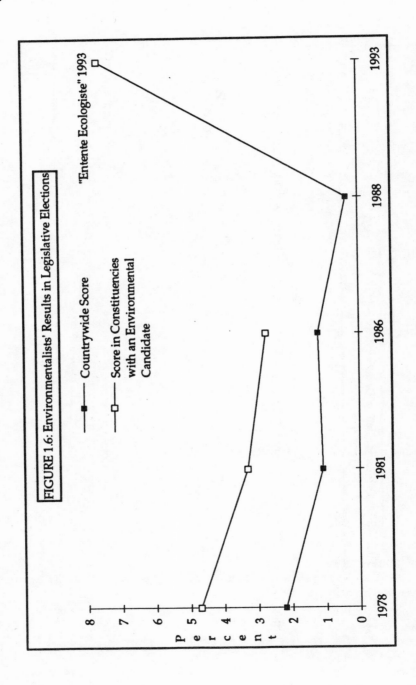

FIGURE 1.6: Environmentalists' Results in Legislative Elections

Notes

1. J. Pignero had in fact campaigned against all forms of radioactivity since 1956. See *Collectif Ecologiste* 1977: 19.

2. See Simonnet 1979; Touraine 1980; Maurice, 1987; Bennahmias and Roche 1992; Pronier and Le Seigneur 1992.

3. We use the term 'civil society' in a similar way to A. Gramsci and A. Gorz. See Chapter 2.

4. PSU: *Parti Socialiste Unifié*. Founded in 1960 as a left-wing opposition to the SFIO (*Section Française de l'Internationale Ouvrière*), the PSU was the most important element in the 'alternative left' and close to environmental concerns.

5. Brice Lalonde is the head of *Génération Ecologie*, founded in May 1990. See below.

6. The Vanoise Park was the first national park created in 1963.

7. The FNSPN brought together the *Ligue pour la Protection des Oiseaux*, the SNPN and numerous regional associations of the same type.

8. This magazine was a pure product of the anarchist culture associated with the movement of May 1968 and very popular with the environmentalists. It has recently reappeared.

9 Anarchist in this book is synonymous with the French term *libertaire* (i.e. appertaining to anarchist political culture).

10. See Vadrot 1978; Allan Michaud 1989; Bennahmias and Roche 1992.

11. In many ways, this lack of transmission between the State and the citizen in France fuelled the burgeoning anti-nuclear movement (see below).

12. See, among others, Illich 1973 and Chapter 3.

13. On the 29 June 1974, the APRE headlined: "Environmentalism will be anarchist (*libertaire*) or nothing at all."

14. "The appeal of 400 scientists: we call on the population to reject nuclear power plants" in *Le Monde*, 11 February 1975. This appeal came from scientists working in the *Collège de France*, in the CEA (*Commissariat à l'Energie Atomique*) and in universities.

15. Leo Kowarski was director of the CEA (*Commissariat à l'Energie Atomique)* from 1946 to 1954.

16. The *Conseil Général* is the elected assembly for the French departments (*départements*). It is made up of different *cantons* and represents an intermediary tier of government between the region and the municipality.

17. The DUP (*déclaration d'utilité publique*) is the government green light for a project which has been through a public enquiry (EUP: *Enquête d'Utilité*

Publique).

18. The fast-breeder reactor, 'Super-Phénix' has a load of 4.6 tons of plutonium and 5,000 tons of liquid sodium.

19. The demonstrators established the first pirate radio station in France (*Radio-Active*) which was immediately banned by the authorities.

20. D. Bernard (*Verts-Bretagne*), interview, 19 June 1990.

21. The project of Le Pellerin went through several changes over the years, including a change of site; i.e. it was moved further down the Loire river to a site called 'Le Carnet'. In 1993, it would seem to have been abandoned.

22. C. Sweet reaches a similar conclusion in comparing the French and British procedures in "A Study of Nuclear Power in France", Energy Paper N° 2, Polytechnic of the South Bank, 1981 in Chafer 1985. The thesis that there exists an influential 'nucleocracy' (*nucléocratie*) reaching into business, politics, the Army and the Civil Service is developed by P. Simonnet in *Les Nucléocrates*. Grenoble, Presses Universitaires de Grenoble. Part One.

23. J. P. Colson makes a study of the public enquiry system in the context of the nuclear power programme in Colson 1977.

24. *Les Amis de la Terre* became the *Réseau des Amis de la Terre* (RAT) in 1977. *Pollution-Non* was created in 1970 and was the fore-runner to the APRE and *Ecologie*.

25. C. Piaget was one of the leaders of the strike at the 'LIP' watch factory in Besançon (Doubs), 1973. This strike became a symbol of self-management theory in practice for the alternative left in general and the PSU in particular.

26. J. F. Kahn is today editor of *L'Evénement du Jeudi*.

27. This was an organization led by Ph. St. Marc, a high ranking civil servant (*fonctionnaire*) which tried to increase environmental awareness in official circles. Ph. St. Marc gave his support to the right-wing candidate, V. Giscard d'Estaing between the two rounds of the 1974 presidential elections.

28. Up to 1989, all election results are first round results. Wherever possible, we present two types of results for each election which was not national (i.e. in which candidates were not present all over the country). Firstly, the total score and total percentage, regardless of where environmental candidates were fielded and, secondly, the percentage of the vote in those places (*communes, cantons,* departments or constituencies) in which environmental candidates were fielded. This second result is the most relevant but political commentators and journalists alike often favour the first. It was rarely possible to obtain the total number of votes cast in those *communes, cantons,* departments or constituencies where environmental candidates were fielded. In most cases, we simply present the percentage score.

29. The ME was strongest in Rhône-Alpes, the south east, the east and the north of the country.

30. There had been cantonal and by-elections in 1976. In certain parts of the

country, the cantonal scores were already promising; Haut-Rhin: 12 percent in Guebwiller, 13 percent in Mulhouse Sud. Yvelines: 12.5 percent in Meulan, 12 percent in Poissy (Dupupet 1984: 283). In the by-elections of November 1976, B. Lalonde and R. Dumont scored 6.5 percent in the fifth Parisian *arrondissement* (Collectif Ecologiste 1977: 35).

31. P. Samuel [RAT] in Vadrot 1978: 96.

32. P. Radanne in Vadrot 1978: 125.

33. Chafer 1985: 8.

34. *Le Front Autogestionnaire* was principally composed of the PSU, the MAN, regionalists, feminists and diverse local, independent environmental groups.

35. This notwithstanding, the percentage vote of environmental candidates in the constituencies where they were fielded -- 4.7 percent -- was over twice as high as the total national percentage -- 2.2 percent (see Table 1.3).

36. The MRG (*Mouvement des Radicaux de Gauche*) was formed in 1972 by a left of center faction of the *Parti Radical* and it supported the *Programme Commun* of the PS and the PC at this time.

37. "from a common 'feeling' (...) to a common political project." *Mouvement d'Ecologie Politique-2*, (Brochure), 1980.

38. That is, 'party men' and bureaucrats.

39. Jean-Claude Demaure, interview, 20 December 1989. C. Demaure is at present a municipal councillor in Nantes (Loire Atlantique).

40. The magazine *Alternatives Economiques* began publishing in 1980.

41. In the French context, it includes three different sectors: a) the cooperatives (production and distribution), b) the mutual aid insurance companies (*mutuelles*), c) the associations which produce a product or a service, normally with salaried members. See "L'Economie sociale, entre étatisation et capitalisme" in *Les Cahiers Français*, N°221, May-June, 1985, pp. 3-4.

42. This was the first cooperative of distribution which remains a historical reference point for many activists in this sector.

43. See "RFA, des banquiers pas comme les autres" in *Alternatives Economiques*, N°30, October 1985.

44. *A Faire* (magazine of ALDEA), N°1, 1982: 12.

45. P. Sauvage, founder member of ALDEA in Allan Michaud 1989: 34.

46. In May 1985, there was a first attempt with the meeting-symposium *Pratiques Alternatives*, organized in order to bring actors on the alternative scene together. Between 1987 and 1988, the attempt was continued with *Arc-en-Ciel* (see below).

47. *Folavoine*, October 1986, p. 4. *Folavoine* is the monthly magazine of the MRJC (*Mouvement Rural de la Jeunesse Chrétienne*).

48. The dual economy is an expression used to designate the division between a highly sophisticated, profitable economic sector and one in which

large sectors of the less qualified classes survive on part-time jobs and increasingly limited unemployment benefits.

49. "Nuclear policy: the government decides to leave EDF's programme alone" in *Le Monde*, 1 August 1981.

50. In the elections to the *équipe fédérale* (executive committee) in February, only one member of the RAT was elected. See Chafer 1984.

51. B. Lalonde in Chafer 1983 [b]. B. Lalonde was once the leading spokesperson for the RAT and in making this statement he has perhaps touched on one of the reasons why he did not take part in the environmentalists' unification process of the early 1980s.

52. At this time, the example of the German Greens (*Die Grünen*) was a major reference point. They were to make a spectacular entry into the German parliament in the following year by winning 5.6 percent of the vote and twenty-seven seats in the Federal elections of March 1983 but already their reputation had crossed frontiers. See Hülsberg 1988.

53. *Lettre-Contact, (Bulletin de liaison des Verts-Confédération Ecologiste-Parti Ecologiste)*, 25 July 1984. *Lettre-Contact* was the name of the internal bulletin of *Les Verts*. It is now called *Vert-Contact*.

54. Cochet Y. 1984: *Contribution à la stratégie et appel à une liste Tocquevilienne* (Text). AGM of *Les Verts*, 1984.

55. For a discussion of the *Rainbow Warrior* affair, see Hanley D. 1986: "The Perils of Grandeur -- Greenpeace, the Socialists and the State" in *Review of the Association for the Study of Modern and Contemporary France*, N° 25, March, pp. 4-10.

56. For these elections, each party presented a list of candidates. The seats available in a constituency were distributed according to the percentage of the vote. Given the high number of seats in this constituency (24) and the good electoral record of the local *Verts*, it was considered that with 5 percent of the vote, a seat was guaranteed.

57. The most important meetings of alternative-environmental activists were as follows: *Pratiques Alternatives*, Paris, 26 May 1985; *Rencontres Ecologie et Mouvement Ouvrier*, Paris, 17 January 1987; *Appel pour un Arc-en-Ciel*, Paris, 18 January 1987; *Premières Assises d'Arc-en-Ciel*, Lyon, 16-18 October 1987; *Deuxièmes Assises d'Arc-en-Ciel*, Paris, 23-24 January 1988; *Forum: Alternative et nouvelle culture politique*, Paris, 19 March 1988.

58. *Appel pour un Arc-en-Ciel* (Text), January, 1987.

59. Interestingly, one of the motions at the AGM of *Les Verts* in June 1993 was entitled 'Social Environmentalism' (*Ecologie Sociale*). The fact that its authors dared to use such a title is a sign of how conceptions of environmentalism are changing.

60. Radanne 1987: *Pour une fécondation de l'écologie et du social* (text of *Arc-en-Ciel*). P. Radanne was one of the initiators of *Arc-en-Ciel* and member of *Les*

Verts.

61. Alain de Swarte is editor of *Combat Nature*, a well-respected environmental magazine .

62. A. Waechter, speech at the AGM of *Les Verts*, November 1986. Personal notes.

63. The TGV (*Train de Grande Vitesse*) is the name of the French high-speed train.

64. M. Gillard, E. Fournier, P.-Y. Maignan, R. Delmas, G. Tordo, F. Fernex, R. M. Allegret, J. Préchaud, G. Roche et J. P. Picaud presented the motion: *Pour un courant fondamentaliste chez Les Verts* (*Vert-Contact* 82 bis, 1988).

65. Bousseau C., Buchmann A., Cambot G., Devoucoux B., Gueydon Y., Hascoët G., Marimot G., Richard-Molard C., Vidal J.-L., Waechter A., 1988: *Motion d'orientation*, AGM des *Verts*, Paris. In *Vert Contact*, N° 82 bis.

66. See Pronier and Le Seigneur 1992. The application for membership of P. Juquin was ratified by the CNIR by a vote of 60.5 percent (60 percent necessary), on the 5 October 1991 (*Vert-Contact* N° 216, 1991). On the attitude of *Les Verts* towards ex-alternative left activists applying for membership, see also, Frémion Y., "Contribution au débat sur les «Rouges et Verts»", *Tribune des Verts*, 22-28 July 1989.

67. Despite the fact that 45 percent of environmentalists live in towns of under 20,000 inhabitants (see Chapter IV).

68. *Le Monde* (23 March 1989) estimated that the environmentalists had won 757 seats in 1983, even if the label 'environmental' was sometimes quite arbitrary at that time.

69. *Ouest France*: 13 March 1989). The rivers in Brittany are polluted, principally, by intensive farming methods.

70. The popular television programme (*La Marche du Siècle*) presented by Jean-Marie Cavada had an environmentalism special (*Planète en Danger*) on the 20 February 1989.

71. Max Siméoni, a Corsican activist and Djida Tazdait, an anti-racist activist from Lyon

72. The conflict which most people expected at the AGM was, however, present at the following internal meeting (i.e. CNIR) when A. Waechter's distribution of party positions was considered highly unfair by the opposition. The journalist from *Le Monde* (21 November 1989) talked of an attempt at an "OPA (*offre publique d'achat*; i.e. an unfriendly take-over bid in Stock Exchange jargon) by A. Waechter on *Les Verts*. A second meeting was necessary.

73. That is, those socialist voters who put the Left into power in 1981 and who consider it has not lived up to its promises.

74. Waechter A; *Heure de Vérité* (Antenne 2 Television), 3 February 1992

75. This agency brought together the AFME (*Agence Française pour la Maîtrise de l'Energie*), the AQA (*Agence pour la Qualité de l'Air*) and the ANRED

(*Agence Nationale pour la Récupération et l'Elimination des Déchets*). It eventually saw the light of day on the 2 of April 1992 with Mr Moussel (ex-PSU) at its head, Mr Denby-Wilkes as Director, 600 employees and a first year budget of 840 million Francs.

76. See Pronier and Le Seigneur 1992: Chapter 8.

77. Motion signed by A. Waechter (among others): *L'Ecologie, une philosophie de partage*. AGM, *Les Verts*: Strasbourg, November 1990. (voted by 44.8 percent)

78. Pacifism in French has a very negative connotation as it evokes memories of the Munich Treaty of 1938.

79. The Somport tunnel is to be built between France and Spain.

80. This meeting took place in Paris, 26-27 September 1992.

81. B. Lalonde head of *Génération Ecologie*, was wholeheartedly for the Maastricht Treaty; Waechter and half *Les Verts* were critically positive and the other half (e.g. D. Voynet, A. Lipietz and M.-C. Blandin) were totally against, considering that the Maastricht Treaty of European Union represented a purely economic vision of Europe which totally neglected the social and environmental dimensions. In the event, the Treaty was accepted in France by 51.05 percent of the votes cast. Within *Génération Ecologie* and *Les Verts*, it was estimated that 61 percent of the former and 57 percent of the latter voted in favour.

82. The surveys on voting intentions were carried out by BVA and CSA, two of the principal survey organisations in France.

83. L. Fabius was replaced by M. Rocard as the Socialist Party's leader following the elections in what some saw as a 'palace coup'.

84. There were unpublished polls in the last week which put the environmental score at 11 percent.

85. See D. Boy, *Le Monde*, 8 April 1993.

86. The creation of *Les Verts* in January 1984 brought together *Les Verts-Parti Ecologiste* and *Les Verts-Confédération Ecologiste*.

87. The first environmentalist to contest elections did so at the legislative elections in Mulhouse in 1973.

2

Environmentalists and Political Culture in France

The aim of this chapter is to explore the political dimension of culture with regard to French environmentalism. What do we mean by political culture and how far can we speak of an environmental political culture?

From Culture to Political Culture

The concept of culture is central to the social sciences in that "man is the culturebearing and culturecreating animal" (Tucker 1973: 174) and this universal importance in the study of human action no doubt explains the plethora of definitions. A. L. Kroeber and Clyde Kluckohn unearthed no less than one hundred and sixty-four definitions of which E. Tylor's remains the most famous:

> that complex whole which includes knowledge, belief, art, morals, custom, and any other capabilities and habits acquired by man as a member of society[1]

Universally important as the study of culture may be in human action, two ostensibly paradoxical interpretations can be given to it. The first is that which revolves around the notion of the constraining force as visible in the writings of Emile Durkheim and Talcott Parsons. This maintains that society's culture is a force which moulds its individuals through a process of socialization. This socialization process includes the transmission of the social norms and values that need to be adopted for society to function correctly. The alternative interpretation is one which considers culture to be a force of liberation for human beings in that it enables them to develop their abilities of learning and creation. It will be shown that two similar interpretations may be given to political culture.

Political Culture

As a concept, political culture has a relatively short history. It was first used by G. Almond in 1956 (Almond 1956) and opened the way for a wealth of literature on the importance of the relationship between cultural and political behavior. That is to say that the purely structural explanations of political behavior (e.g. institutions, systems) were to be subsequently considered as insufficient and, as a result, more subjective, personal factors (e.g. individual psychology, symbolism) were considered necessary to complete the analysis. Put another way, the introduction of political culture into the realm of political theory allowed the gap between macro (political system) and micro (individual) analysis to be bridged even if it also introduced an accompanying pitfall of extrapolation from the individual to the collective, or the collective to the individual. Despite this potential pitfall it remains an important element in the formation of any social movement and any difficulties encountered in its delineation could be a clue to the difficulties of the movement in question to assert itself in the political arena.

From the outset, the concept of political culture was seen as being distinct from the wider general culture of a nation or people. This distinction existed in the eyes of G. Almond who considered that the former constituted a society's "pattern of orientation to political action, which is a differentiated part of the culture and has a certain autonomy" (Tucker 1973: 175). This idea of an autonomous political sphere within society reflected the theoretical origins of the concept; i.e. functional-systems analysis. The general culture of a society was seen by functionalists as the "skin or fabric of a society, binding together not only its individual members but its major institutions by providing a common set of goals and values" (Slattery 1985: 19). That is to say a form of core culture from which other sub-cultures were derived. It is within this idea of a dominant, consensual vision of the cultural order that the concept of political culture came into being. The concept was to have a specific function, that is, to be used as an explanation of the essentially psychological dimension of the political system, the latter being seen as a semi-independent functioning system within the more global social system.

To view political culture in this light is insufficient and may even be considered misleading in that culture as a general, anthropological concept takes stock of both the psychological and behavioral aspects of human activity. Would it not be possible for political culture to do the same? It is at this point that the difference in the interpretation and usage of this concept becomes clear. It is one which may be defined in different ways and the implications in the choice made are fundamental.[2]

a) Objective. This interpretation of political culture revolves around the Parsonian concept of culture which is central to his view of the social system. The 'patterns of culture' which shape social actors' behavior are part of the 'object world' and are formed by what he terms "cultural objects": "cultural objects are the laws, ideas, and so forth, as the actor-subject sees these things outside himself. The same laws and ideas may eventually become internalized elements of culture for the actor-subject; *as such* they will not be cultural objects but components of the actor-subject's system of action" (Patrick 1978: 5; author's emphasis). This means that culture is firstly an external object which, once learnt by a member of society through the process of socialization, becomes internalized and an integral part of his behavioral patterns. The extension into the realms of politics was made by David Easton for whom political culture was, principally, a means to study the relationship of social actors to their political system. More specifically, it was seen as a manner of analyzing the normative and value standards that regulate political behavior and maintain the stability of the political system in which it takes place:

> [political culture] consists of the total constellation of beliefs or ideas
> about the structure of authority, norms (rules and laws), values (goals

and purpose), and symbols that are authoritatively enforced either through appeal to a formal constitution or to tradition or a set of informal customs and habits, deviation from which results in authoritative sanctions or informal sanctions (Patrick 1978: 9).

Such a preoccupation with maintenance and stability within the political realm echoes that of Parsons' more general concern with regard to culture in the social one. The principal feature in this 'objective' interpretation of political culture is that the latter is external to the individual and is forced upon him by the controlling agents of society (e.g. education and norms) and is reminiscent of Durkheim's notion of social facts that exist independently of the individual (Durkheim, 1896)

b) *Psychological-Subjective.* Almond and Verba's interpretation of political culture (Almond and Verba 1963) was different in that they considered it to be an internal phenomenon, forming a part of the individual's personality system. It differs therefore from Parson's and Easton's 'objective' interpretation in that it is something which is acquired by the individual through a psychological process as opposed to a purely sociological one. It is for this reason that Patrick terms it the 'subjective-psychological' definition. For the two aforementioned authors, political culture was the "subjective realm which underlies and gives meaning to political action" (Patrick 1978: 10), and this definition is the one which has held most sway in the political sciences since the inception of the concept. It is a definition which is reminiscent of the 'Thomas Theorem'[3] in that what is considered as important is less the reality of the political world than what people believe of it: "As Verba notes, the political 'refers not to what is happening in the world of politics, but what people believe about those happenings' " (Patrick 1978: 13). What becomes important in such an interpretation are the perceptions, feelings and thoughts of people with regard to their political worlds, even if these perceptions, feelings and thoughts are partly a result of the political system in which they are to be found. It maintains, nevertheless, that the key features of a political system are to be discovered in the orientations of individuals and that these orientations constitute its defining or distinctive characteristics.

Although these two interpretations may seem different they have a common interest; i.e. individual integration into the political system via the internalization process:

> When we speak of the political culture of a society, we refer to the political system as internalized in the cognitions, feelings and evaluations of its population. People are inducted into it just as they are socialized into non-political roles and social systems. (Patrick 1978: 10)

c) Comprehensive. The third interpretation of political culture is the one which receives the least attention by G. Patrick and this is unfortunate as we believe it is the one which offers the most empirical and theoretical potential.

The authors who are associated with this comprehensive interpretation are R. Tucker and R. Fagen.[4] Both these authors suggest that the objective and psychological definitions are too limited as they only take into account what people think, feel or believe. The comprehensive definition of political culture is one which goes a step further by stating that it is necessary to also study the recurring patterns of behavior which are the outcome of the aforementioned feelings. In the same way as Ralph Linton speaks about "overt" and "covert" forms of culture in a society[5], the comprehensive interpretation of political culture returns to the anthropological approach to general culture by encompassing psychological and behavioral patterns. We believe this interpretation offers the most latitude in the study of a social movement as what people think and believe is, of course, of fundamental importance but what they then go on to do is as much so.

Functions of Political Culture

The functions of political culture are twofold. Firstly, from the standpoint of the individual, the political culture of a society gives meaning and substance to the political system in which he or she operates. From the standpoint of the political system, its internalization, voluntarily or otherwise, has been seen as a means of integrating individuals into the body politic. In this respect, the first function is one of regulating the political behavior of political and non-political actors in an acceptable way for the maintenance and stability of the system in question. Clearly, political culture in this light has a constraining effect on political behavior and this is, indeed, congruent with the majority of theoretical discussion around this concept, conceived, as we have noted, within the Functionalist womb of American sociology.

However, a second function is also possible. One which contains a liberating dimension. One which permits a social movement to construct a different vision of society that questions its social and political foundations and to act upon it. One which includes the cognitive and behavioral aspects of human action and which we would define as: *that whole which contains the beliefs, myths, symbols, references, events, language, humor, art, and observable behavioral patterns of a community and/or social movement which are associated with it and, consciously or unconsciously, reflected by it.*

It is a concept which has empirical content in that certain elements, such as beliefs and behavioral patterns for example, can be analyzed and, to a certain extent, measured. The concept need not, therefore, exercise a purely constraining function in the political process and can serve at least three different functions. Firstly, as a descriptive tool of reference. Secondly as an explanatory tool of analysis and, thirdly, as a basis for action. Political culture is a fundamental and necessary element of any social movement. Such a movement, if the term is to retain any meaning, has to distinguish itself from others which may also contain aims of social transformation. The development stage of its autonomous political culture is an indicator of its political maturity and as a logical corollary to this, any difficulty in delineating this specific, autonomous political culture could begin to explain the difficulties encountered by such a movement in making social and/or political advances.

Before considering the nature of environmental political culture and the development stage it has reached, a preliminary discussion on the nature of the surrounding national political culture of the Fifth French Republic is necessary.

French Political Culture:
Nationalism, Republicanism and the State

The year of 1989 was the bicentenary of the French Revolution, a revolution which constituted, arguably, the most important single historical event of the last two hundred years in Europe. This appreciation aside, its social and political legacy is enormous and still shapes French society. This revolution, based on a combination of Cartesian rationalism and Rousseauist patriotism, carried nationalism far beyond that of England in the 17th century by replacing royal, ecclesiastical power with a new form of civic religion based on individual and collective faith in the Republic. This new found faith gave rise to the first national education system designed to raise patriotic citizens ready to defend the Nation and its Universal Declaration of Human Rights. This first aggressive manifestation of nationalism as a political force had the most important effect of totally identifying the individual with the newly-born State. The comparison made by Hans Kohn between the English and French traditions of nationalism clarifies this:

> the [English] nation-state was regarded as a protective shell for the free interplay of individual forces. The nationalism of the French Revolution *stressed that the duty and dignity of the citizen lay in political activity and his fulfillment in complete union with his nation-state.* (Kohn 1971: 23). [6]

This intimate, and at times ambiguous relationship of the citizen to the State is at the heart of French political culture and has shaped social and political action ever since.

Republicanism in French political culture is a tradition which both left and right wings today lay claim to. The mainstream left, in particular, has always seen the State apparatus as the means to 'put society the right way up', to paraphrase Marx's opinion of Hegelian dialectics. The State was the instrument to be used in the necessary social change once it arrived in power and could finish the job the Jacobins had started.[7] It is a tradition which, from the initial victory of the Jacobins over the Girondins, sees society in terms of a monolithic block at the top of which stands the necessarily strong executive power. The creation of a centralizing State apparatus was one which inspired national (Napoleon) and international (Lenin) leaders alike but the short and long-term effects of it are reminiscent of the 'Two Watersheds' theory of I. Illich (Illich 1973). That is, the first watershed (i.e. the French Revolution) was extremely beneficial in eradicating illiteracy, improving conditions of public health and extending franchising rights to the general (male) population, to mention but a few. The second was perhaps less so in that the centralizing State subsequently acquired such power as to become untouchable for oppositional movements and the environmentalists are no exception to this. It can, of course, be claimed that centralism is a feature of any advanced industrial State and, therefore, presents difficulties to every national environmental movement. It would seem, however, that the Jacobin and subsequent Napoleonic legacies[8] have produced a particularly powerful form of political, economic and social centralism which flies in the face of two important environmental tenets; autonomy and diversity. It is highly possible that this centralizing tradition in all aspects of life has brought about two lasting consequences from which the environmentalists, as others, have suffered.

The first is to render the citizen both largely powerless in the face of, but dependent on, central authority, thereby creating a form of individual *unempowerment* (*déresponsabilisation*) aggravated by the individualism inherent to any consumer society. That is to say that, in the absence of sufficiently powerful intermediary bodies between the citizen and the State (e.g. a strong and autonomous 'civil society') oppositional collective action very soon comes up against State structures and the immensity of overcoming this structural obstacle can discourage the most willing of social actors. This could go towards explaining why social change in France is often a result of major confrontation. François de Beaulieu (ex-*Vert*) summed this up by saying that "France is a country which moves forwards in bursts. We have a revolution, put the lid back on and wait for the next explosion" (interview). Such a context makes life difficult for the environmental movement which is striving for profound, long-term changes in individual and collective behavior.

The second consequence, a corollary of the first, is visible in the weakness of French 'civil society'. The term civil society is often associated with the Italian Marxist, Antonio Gramsci and definitions vary:

- a whole range of structures and activities like Trade Unions, schools, the Churches and the family. (Boggs 1976: 39)
- between the coercive relations of the State and the economic sphere of production lies civil society, namely that area of life which *appears* as the realm of the private citizen and individual consent. (Abercrombie, Hill and Turner 1988: 34; authors' emphasis)

The French eco-socialist, A. Gorz extended this to mean:

the web of social relationships that individuals establish between themselves in groups or communities which are neither the result of mediation nor any institutional act of the State; they are relationships of a voluntary and reciprocal nature, not of law and legal obligation (Gorz 1978: 46)

In contemporary France, civil society is best illustrated by associational life. This sector is weak because too few citizens are involved and because it is subordinated to political and administrative institutions. Within the confines of our discussion, a good example of this is to be found in a comparison of European environmental organizations.[9]

The environmental associations in France have much less room to maneuver than their European counterparts as Table 2.1 indicates. This is so because they are tied to the political powers, whether left or right: "The statutes of *France-Nature-Environnement* reveal that its members do not themselves have the power to modify the association or even its statutes: any such decisions made during an AGM have to be sent to the relevant Minister and are only valid subject to government approval. Ministerial authorities also vet the code of practice and all the association's official acts (e.g. registers, accounts, annual reports) as well as the way in which certain resources emanating from government administrations are used. These are a good example of statutes imposed upon associations which have received the government seal of approval [*associations reconnues d'utilité publique*]." (Chibret 1991: 729)[10]

TABLE 2.1   European Associations for Environmental
            Protection

	BN[a] Germany	AT[b] France	FNE[c] France	RSPB[d] G.-B.
Membership (thousands)	77	1.6	25	850
Turnover (thousands)	6 450 DM[e]	320 Fr	3 600 Fr	£27 800
Subsidies (Percent)	7	48	60	nil

[a] AT: *Amis de la Terre.*
[b] BN: *Bund Naturschutz.*
[c] FNE: *France Nature Environnement.* The FNE is the ex-FFSPN. Figures for membership vary considerably. We have based ours on Chibret 1991.
[d] RPSB: Royal Society for the Protection of Birds. Data of September 1992.
[e] DM = Deutschmark, Fr = French Francs. 1$ = 5.8 Francs, 1 Deutschmark = 3.4 Francs, £1 = 8.7 Francs (December 1993).

Sources: Chibret 1991; RPSB information service 1992.

This quotation sums up the dilemma of most associations which do not have the financial or political autonomy necessary to be taken seriously. The political powers can, on the other hand, use this sector to channel popular discontent and even to make up for shortcomings within the public sector in time of need.[11] On a more general plane of analysis, the sociologist Serge Moscovici has drawn attention to the attraction which many associations have in France to "institutions" in order to survive: "It's true that in France, you cannot escape from the power of institutions; even associations, either because of ideological control or economic dependence, tend to hide behind official institutions" (Moscovici 1985). Patrick Viveret reached similar conclusions in speaking of the way in which decisions in France begin at the top of the State structure and eventually filter down to civil society.[12] Unfortunately, it is precisely within this civil society, and associational life in particular, that the environmentalists place their hopes. The associational sector is often seen as a possible base within which their movement could develop.

A final aspect of this discussion on the role of the State and its institutions is to be found in its formidable power of integration of opposition. Two examples of this are the personal careers of F. Mitterrand and B. Lalonde, both of whom were critics of the Fifth Republic before being painlessly integrated into it. This is to say that oppositional discourse which is not integrated in some way (e.g. by a major party or a minister in office) has great difficulty in surviving and the experience of *Génération Ecologie* (launched while B. Lalonde was in government) is revealing in this respect. Given this background, the fact that the environmentalists have managed to survive into the 1990s is a feat in itself.

The Electoral System

This discussion of French political culture would be incomplete without a look at the electoral system and how the environmentalists cope with it.

Any political group which wishes to be taken seriously as a political force in the country is obliged to take part in presidential elections as the whole of political life is structured around them. Elections to this office, however, do not lend themselves to political breakthrough. In the first place, each candidate needs 500 signatures from the *grands électeurs*.[13] Quite obviously, the major parties do all in their power to prevent their members supporting rival candidates and this first hurdle is often enough to dissuade minority candidates. Secondly, presidential election campaigns are very expensive and in order to afford them a prospective candidate must have a large, well-organized and above all well-resourced political movement behind him or her. This has not been the case for the environmentalists who have often been obliged to rely on subscriptions, sporadic donations and bank loans for the bulk of their income during different electoral campaigns.[14] Thirdly, the two-round voting system means that the real choice for the elector is usually reduced to a straight choice between two candidates, one of the right and one of the left, in the second round. Fourthly, the voting system leads, inevitably, to the personalization of presidential election campaigns. Given the lack of air time generally accorded to the leader of a minority political group outside election periods and the consequent difficulty for its leader to establish her/himself as a national figure, this has been a major problem for the environmentalists. Furthermore, this very process of over-personalization is a constant preoccupation of the movement, reflecting its anarchist strand of thought and practice (see Chapter 3). The environmental movement in general, and *Les Verts* in particular, aspire towards practising a different kind of politics. This has meant the creation of structures specifically designed to avoid the over-personalization of control and the centralization of power within the movement. Consequently, the nature of the Fifth French Republic has always, at least implicitly, been put into question. Indeed, in their 1981 publication (Aujourd'hui L'Ecologie: 1981), they advocated the creation of a Sixth Republic in which the parliamentary process would dominate the executive power:

> The powers of the president have to be reduced. He should preside over the State as he does at present but he should be the arbitrator between society and the State, a lawyer for society against the State. The government should answer, as before, to parliament (*Aujourd'hui L'Ecologie* 1981: 250 - 251)

This original hostility to the dominant political system has evolved over the years as the participation in elections illustrates, although it has not disappeared altogether, and constitutes one of the many environmental paradoxes; how to participate in a system, the very nature of which they disagree with but with which the French population seems to be quite satisfied? (Gaffney 1988)

A fifth problem faced by the environmentalists in this type of election is the 5 percent barrier to the reimbursement of election campaign expenses, a threshold which they consistently failed to reach.[15] Despite the cost, and the fact that there is no hope of winning, the environmentalists have felt obliged to participate and have come to consider a presidential election campaign as a useful public platform for publicizing environmental ideas to a mass audience.

It is not only in presidential elections that institutional representation is virtually impossible for minority political movements. The system of two-round voting for legislative elections, with all candidates who have not reached a 12.5 percent threshold in the first round being eliminated, works very much to the disadvantage of new or small political groups which have no hope of election without the support of one of the major established parties. In practice, the second round of voting is thus usually reduced to a straight contest between the best placed candidates of the right and the left and this tradition has contributed to a voters' perception that the first round of elections is largely irrelevant, or at least of only secondary significance. Given that, up to 1993, environmentalists were never present in the second round,[16] their credibility has not been enhanced by this type of election.

The environmentalists have, therefore, tended to focus their hopes for political representation on those elections which involve a proportional voting system. These include the regional, European and to a lesser extent municipal elections,[17] each of which appear to offer better hopes of success. Indeed, it was in the municipal elections of 1989, and especially in the following European elections, that the environmentalists made their most important electoral gains to date.

This presentation of certain salient features of French political culture highlights two points of interest. Firstly, the strategy of the conquest of power is necessarily vertical. The right and left wings in French politics have concentrated their strategy on the capture of central, Parisian, State power. In doing so they have perpetuated a political socialization process that renders the citizen almost totally dependent on the institutions of the State and/or one of the two political blocks. The consequences of this are twofold. Firstly, it gives rise to a relatively closed political opportunity structure, thereby creating a form of *unempowerment* on the part of the citizen who finds her/himself with few possibilities of effective collective action other than direct confrontation with State structures. Secondly, it creates a separation between the political sphere and civil society, between which there are few intermediaries. This centralizing vision of social organization is one which was very effective at eradicating structural inequalities in a relatively uncomplicated social context. It is however, less than adequate in a highly complex social organization in which the flow and control of information is a dominant feature. Such an information-based society needs to be flexible in its responses to social demands. The Fifth French Republic has been anything but and the events of May 1968 could be seen as the first cracks appearing in the social edifice. The May 1968 generation, as we have seen, played a major role in the genesis of the environmental movement.

Secondly, the electoral system remains hostile to the environmentalists, among others. The founding of the Fifth French Republic by General de Gaulle in 1958 was ostensibly motivated by a desire to avoid the political instability of the Fourth Republic. An institutional framework was thus devised which tended to strengthen the power of the executive at the expense of the legislature, a tendency which was further reinforced by the interventionist style of de Gaulle and the change to electing the President by universal suffrage in 1962. The executive has thus emerged as the most important centre of power in the country and the presidency as the most significant elected political office under its Constitution.[18] The accompanying electoral system is a reflection of this situation and goes a long way to explaining the difficulties faced by the environmentalists over the years even if this purely structural element is insufficient as a total explanation. What it does, however, is to institutionalize a political divide between the left and right blocks at each election, thereby eradicating minority groups.

Environmental Political Culture

How valid is it to talk of an environmental political culture and, if the latter exists, what does it consist of? Three aspects stand out in this discussion. Firstly, the environmental myth. How is it constructed and what are its symbols and references? Secondly, the political and cultural practices of environmental militants. How far have *Les Verts* managed to put into practice their ideas of 'alternative politics'? What role does lifestyle play in a movement which wishes to build a "cultural majority" (A.

Waechter)? Finally, what is the importance of the environmental political identity and how has it been constructed?

Myths, Symbols and References

The Environmental Myth.

Forceful ideas rather than purely false ones, the social importance of myths is due to their capacity to mobilize sentiment behind a dynamic process which, in itself, brings about real effects (Braud 1985: 35).[19]

Everybody needs myths. The advent of Rationalism did not do away with them, it simply replaced them with others (e.g. technology). Myths could be seen as the translation of hope into reality. Their principal function is to mobilize people as opposed to explaining or interpreting the world, as was the case in more primitive societies. These are some of the universal aspects of myths and an autonomous political culture needs its own. The Socialist movement had its myths, the most tenacious of which was, no doubt, that of the dictatorship of the proletariat along with that of the 'General Strike', herald of the Revolution, as portrayed by Georges Sorel (1847 - 1922). The environmental myth, somewhat paradoxical in parts, is best summed up in the well-known slogan: "Think globally, act locally".

One of the founding myths of the French Republic was that of the Nation, incarnated by the people (*le peuple*) which was made up of free, equal and brotherly citizens. This myth of the Nation-State is today ascribed to by both the right and the left in French politics. The environmentalists' reply to this mythical backbone of French political culture is to present an alternative myth which shoots off in two different directions. The first direction is global (i.e. the planet) and the second more local (i.e. region, town and village).

Environmental consciousness replaces the nation by the planet, thereby creating the myth of 'spaceship earth' or 'Mother Earth'. To attempt to analyze environmental problems within national limits is the worst possible solution as was demonstrated by the refusal of the radioactive cloud from Chernobyl to stop at the customs barrier. Our 'common house' is now the planet and this shift in consciousness began with the first photos of the earth from outer space. 'Mother earth', the matrix of all life, has taken over from the 'Fatherland' figure of the nation and also given rise to the 'Gaia' hypothesis (Lovelock 1986).[20]

The other side of the environmental mythical coin brings us back down to earth, as it were; back to our own backyard and to things manageable. Local proximity and human scale are the indispensable complements to the 'Mother Earth' dimension, both of which can be summed up by the title of F. Schumacher's famous book, *Small is Beautiful* (Schumacher 1973). Small may be beautiful but, above all, it is controllable in the eyes of environmentalists and this underlying idea is at the heart of their theories on human action: the smaller an activity, the more manageable it is likely to be and the effects can be seen in different domains:

1) Technical; the critique of 'technocratic' projects by the environmentalists can be more easily understood in this light. A highway project, for example, no doubt spoils the view of the countryside as well as developing the importance of the car in society. But it is also a case of the citizen being literally and metaphorically overtaken by a project. The hostility to certain dam projects also represents a mixture of environmental opposition and a refusal to accept technically gigantic projects which swamp the individual.

2) Political; environmentalists' wishes for greater public participation in the decision-making process can be hampered by large-scale projects. The fear is that the larger a project, and the more expensive it is, the less likely it is that the opinions of individual citizens will be taken into account. In the end result, the environmental critique at this point is centred on the power of 'technocrats' in contemporary society. The technocrat is that "functionary [who] tends to concentrate on the technical dimensions of a problem as opposed to its social and human consequences."[21]

3) Social; the idea of the local community is at the heart of environmental thought and action but it can give rise to a fundamental ambivalence in interpretation. When the leader of *Les Verts*, A. Waechter, came to power in 1986, he did so

brandishing this myth: "The community, and especially the small rural community, is the focal point of the society which we aspire to. To forget this would be a profound mistake."[22]

This image of the small rural community has been heavily contested within (and outside) *Les Verts* but it is an interesting one as it ties up with a fundamental sociological problem: how do individuals form a society? How can social solidarity be maintained? These questions are even more acute in today's increasingly individualised and atomised society. The major sociologists who contributed to the birth of Sociology all touched on this question. In 1887, the German sociologist Tönnies referred to "Gemeinschaft" (community) and "Gesellschaft" (association/society) to distinguish between traditional and modern society. Traditional society was one of proximity and 'mechanical solidarity (Emile Durkheim: 1885 - 1917). Modern, complex society is based on the notion of contract (Henry S. Maine: 1822 - 1888), heterogeneity (Herbert Spencer: 1820 - 1903), rational bureaucracy (Max Weber: 1864 - 1920) and 'organic solidarity' (Durkheim). This toing and froing between two types of social organisation is still a part of environmental thinking, between the desire to reconstruct the 'social bond' of past rural communities whilst living in the modern world. The reference to the "small rural community" gives the impression that the environmentalists are leaning backwards but, as ambiguous as such a reference is, it is rather a wish to re-humanise what is seen as a progressively lifeless social body.

These different aspects of the environmental myth help to explain the major anti-nuclear mobilisation of the 1970s. Nuclear technology is gigantic and can only be controlled by a technical elite. The decision-making process is essentially technocratic and nuclear plants need constant police surveillance during normal service and during waste disposal. Several environmentalists claimed they saw the seeds of such a technocratic and police-based society during the incidents of Malville (1977) and Plogoff (1980).

Symbols and References. "Any gesture, artefact, sign or concept which stands for, signifies or expresses something else is a symbol. The study of symbols is important because they are public and convey shared emotions, information or feeling, and may therefore function for social cohesion and commitment." (Abercrombie, Hill and Turner 1988: 248).

The symbolic frame of reference which accompanies the environmental myth is living and natural; the trees and the sun represent the most common allusions. The colours of environmentalism are green and yellow: the former is the colour of plant life and the latter that of the sun, an inexhaustible source of renewable energy. Yellow and green are also the dominant colours of the sunflower used by many European Green parties and illustrating both the attachment to 'Mother Earth' and the renewable energy path of the future (i.e. the sun).

The artefact which best epitomizes environmental theories is the bicycle. The first environmental demonstrations in Paris (1972) were held on bikes and one of the first demands of newly-elected councillors in 1989 was for inner city cycle paths. The bicycle symbolizes the human and non-polluting dimension of an environmental technology and reinforces the emphasis which is laid on the 'soft' nature of environmental human activity in opposition to the 'hardness' of industrialism.

To share the same reading of history is a final aspect of a political culture. The Communists see history as the class struggle. Many Catholics in the north of Ireland see their society as the result of a continuing colonial struggle (the Protestants see it in terms of a battle won in 1690 by William of Orange over the Catholic, James II). Equally, the French environmentalists have their own references which make up their reading of history: Malville (1977), Larzac (1971 - 1981), oil spills, Plogoff (1980), the death of the Portuguese photographer in the attack on the *Rainbow Warrior* (Fernando Pereira, 1985), Chernobyl (1986).

This set of myths, symbols and references makes up the cognitive side of this coin of political culture. The other side is that of behavioral patterns, to which we now turn.

Political and Cultural Practices

For many environmentalists, politics and ethics are virtually synonymous. The main parties are stigmatized because of their undemocratic political procedures and *Les Verts* consider themselves to be the 'Mister Clean' of French politics. Their aims are, however, more ambitious as they consider that individuals must also change their way of life if society is to become more environment-friendly. How far do the activists measure up to these dual aims of adopting alternative political practices within their own organization and leading alternative lifestyles at home?

Political Practices[23].The French environmentalists spent ten long years before they managed to come together under one green umbrella in 1984 (1974: *Mouvement Ecologique* -> 1984: *Les Verts*). In January of that year, the *Confédération Ecologiste* and the *Parti Ecologiste* joined forces and *Les Verts* were born. In the five years that followed, much effort was put into creating an internal structure that could reconcile democracy and efficiency. These efforts were, in part, the reflection of the struggle between the 'anarchists' and the 'organisers' with the latter coming out on top during the institutionalisation of the 1980s. What results have been achieved?

With regard to other parties of the Fifth Republic, *Les Verts* have managed certain fundamental political innovations, some of which are flagging, while others have weathered well. They all concern internal democracy.

Oligarchy? The first innovation is the creation of the CNIR (*Conseil National Inter-Regional*). The CNIR is the supreme decision-making body and is a reflection of the dual concerns for internal democracy and regionalism. Consequently, 75 percent of the delegates are elected by autonomous regional federal sections of the party and 25 percent during the AGM. The Executive College, which includes the four national spokepersons, is subsequently elected by the CNIR. The CNIR is a real innovation within the party system of the Fifth Republic as no other party has gone so far in an attempt to counter R. Michels 'Iron Law of Oligarchy'.[24]

In a similar democratic vein, members have the possibility of organising an internal referendum on any issue, subject to 10 percent support within the party. This internal system is also put forward as a general political proposition in the programme of *Les Verts* (RIP: *Référendum d'Initiative Populaire*) as a means of democratizing French society even though certain commentators remain skeptical as to its feasibility (Pronier and Le Seigneur 1992: 75).

Electoral Mandates. A second innovation concerns electoral mandates. *Les Verts* have adopted a system of 'rotating mandates' which allows, indeed obliges, elected party members to step down in mid-term in favour of their electoral 'co-pilot'. This is to say that for each elected office, two party members stand at (certain) elections and, if they are elected, they share the post. The first example of the system in action was in December 1991 when the EMPs elected in 1989 stood down for their elected partners. The aim behind this is to prevent the over-professionalisation of environmental politics. Time, along with other electoral responsibilities, will tell whether such principles can overcome the necessity of forming an experienced political personnel which is the main argument against this system.

A second barrier against professionalisation is to forbid party members collecting elected posts.[25] Each post is given a number of points and no member can go above 10 points (e.g. municipal councillor of a small town = 1 point, mayor of a town of more than 100,000 inhabitants = 5 points, etc.).

Primaries. The organisation of internal primaries for the presidential elections is another innovation which has even begun to interest other parties (e.g. RPR). These primaries have been held once (4 April - 25 May, 1987) in nine different places,[26] allowing members to question and choose their candidate. The victor at this time was A. Waechter (58.8 percent) over Y. Cochet (28.7 percent) and J. Brière (12.5 percent). Given the importance of presidential elections in French political life, the winner of such a contest also gains added prestige, and therefore power, within the party.[27]

Sexual Equality. Sexual equality is one of the most basic environmental principles. Unfortunately, it often remains just a principle given that women are, in general, less politically active than men (between 1987 and 1989, 26 percent of *Les Verts* were female). Moreover, France is somewhat behind in this domain: "It is well known that France has one of the most misogynous political classes in Europe. Despite the declared intentions of political leaders since the 1970s, we are still waiting for the feminization of national representation." [28]

Within this context, the French environmentalists took longer than their German counterparts in taking this question seriously. At the AGM of 1990 (Strasbourg), however, a motion designed to institutionalize sexual equality was passed and in meetings *Les Verts* often apply what they call the 'zipper' technique; i.e. alternating male and female speeches.

Annual General Meetings and Political Behavior

When these different structural elements of the environmental political culture are lined up, it appears clear that the will exists to make a break with the traditions of the dominant political class. They do not all function perfectly but the desire, in form at least, to practise politics in an alternative manner is certainly present. When it comes down to content, however, alternative politics and alternative political behavior sometimes have trouble coexisting. The best place to witness this is at an annual general meeting (AGM), of which we have experienced ten (1983 - 1992). On such occasions, environmental conviviality can sometimes be sliced up by well-sharpened knives.

Manifest and Latent Functions. Any AGM takes in what R. Merton calls manifest and latent functions. (Merton, 1957). The two manifest functions of AGMs of *Les Verts* are, firstly, to vote the motions for the coming year presented by the party 'heavyweights' (e.g. Anger, Brière, Cochet, Fernex, Hascoët, Marimot, Tête, Voynet, Waechter) and secondly, to elect the CNIR. The latent functions, as the term suggests, are less visible but equally, if not more, important.

(1) Motions. Each motion[29] which is presented represents a long haul for the author (or authors) who needs to enlist the support of several activists around the country. The manifest aim of a motion is, of course, to persuade other activists to follow the political direction indicated in it. The important latent function is to demonstrate the state of play in the internal power struggle by displaying the support given to the motion. This support is visible in both the number of individual activists who

countersign it, by their standing (i.e. if they are well-known figures) and, also, by the number of votes it receives.

In the first two years of *Les Verts'* existence, the well-known orator and organizer, Yves Cochet, was firmly at the helm of the environmental ship. His two successive motions (*Contributions à la stratégie et appel à la constitution d'une liste Tocquevilienne* and *Devenir*) had majority backing. In 1986, however, things were very different when the outgoing leadership (Motion *Construire*: Anger, Cochet, Marimot and Brière) was opposed by the relatively unknown regional councillor, Antoine Waechter[30] who put forward a motion (*Affirmer l'identité politique des écologistes*) that has subsequently become a major point of environmental reference due to its second subtitle: "Environmentalism should not be wed" (*L'écologie n'est pas à marier*). He accused the outgoing leadership of too much contact with the alternative left and of wishing to form a "cartel" for the forthcoming presidential (1988) and municipal (1989) elections. For his own part, he preferred to await the environmental 'coming':

Is it not clear that environmental problems will soon be on the agenda of every industrialised country as we approach the end of this millennium, and that the public will first of all put their faith in environmentalists to solve them? We refuse to put our future in jeopardy through impatience or lassitude. The French electorate will eventually react in a similar way to the Belgian, Swiss, Austrian and German ones even if important institutional and cultural differences remain in its way. (Waechter 1986)

The situation was a perfect example of the aforementioned 'Thomas theorem'; i.e. the fact that the *Construire* motion made no suggestion of creating an electoral cartel was less important than the impression given to the activists that the outgoing leadership was 'selling out' to the alternative left. This meant that the sacred principle of environmental political autonomy was at stake which was enough for the leaders to be voted out.

This AGM is today considered to represent the *'environmentaliste'* turning point of *Les Verts* (i.e. they decided to concentrate more on natural issues than on social ones) and was the scene of a monumental struggle on the evening of Saturday, 8 November 1986. Several attacks had been levelled at the 'IDE'[31] before G. Marimot got up to defend the *Construire* motion. He felt the hostility in the hall and was relatively conciliatory but that was not enough to prevent the explosion which had been brewing. This came about during a discussion over voting procedure and the ensuing pandemonium was such that it needed the intervention of a prestigious invited guest, Daniel Brélaz,[32] to take the meeting in hand. When the main protagonists, Waechter and Cochet, were eventually able to put their cases forward, the former won hands down (65.3 percent).

This tragicomedy stands out amongst green AGMs and reveals the kind of difficulty *Les Verts* have had, and still have, in managing conflict within their organisation. "Differences do not prevent unity, cooperation and efficiency. Environmentalism teaches us that well-managed diversity is a source of stability and security" is the way one activist put it, when referring to the dangers of the National Front (*Tribune Verte*, N°10, November 1990). Another longstanding activist, Michel Bernard, phrased it differently back in 1984 at the first AGM of *Les Verts* by stating that "In France, we look for what is likely to divide us before what may unite us". Be that as it may, in this kind of atmosphere, the cool, calm and collected A. Waechter stood out in 1986. Now and again, certain activists are "dismayed by the verbal violence and personal attacks" (P. Bridier: AGM, 1988) and though the applause to such statements is always heavy, the pause is equally short-lived.

A second major function of an AGM, green or otherwise, is that of political socialisation. Any fresh activist needs to experience an AGM (or a CNIR) in order to feel the pulse of the party. Given that a high percentage of environmentalists, within *Les Verts* at least, are what may be called 'political virgins' in that they have never been active in any other political organisation and given the high turnover rate within this party, it is quite possible that the internal party atmosphere frightens some people away. When we asked a question on this subject in 1988 (*Why do you think Les Verts have not, so far, been successful in France?*), thirty percent of replies suggested that the negative image the general public had of internal political practices was a major handicap. Some activists had already understood this point in 1986: "We must understand that if we continue to be as unconvivial in our meetings, if we continue to squabble amongst ourselves in the newspapers, if we continue to maintain that we are the only ones who ever get it right then we will never bring together people other than dogmatic idealists or dreamers".[33]

With regard to the internal balance of forces that is reflected in the votes of motions, it is clear that there has been a change within *Les Verts* since A. Waechter gained control in 1986 (see Figure. 2.1 at the end of this chapter). Up until 1988, Waechter was in firm control. Between 1989 and 1991, opposition became more visible, albeit unorganized. The principal opposition came from the 'social environmentalism' wing (e.g. Voynet, Cochet, Anger, Hascoët) with a second tendency called *'Fil Vert'* also making an appearance.[34] At the AGM of 1992 (Chambéry, 13 - 15 December) however, the 'dynamic' D. Voynet[35] ran the environmental leader very close by taking 45.1 percent of the vote as opposed to his 51.1 percent.

(2) The Elections to the CNIR. The direct elections to the CNIR represent the second manifest function of the AGM of *Les Verts*. These elections are held under a system of proportional representation in which different lists of names are put up for election and they are considered important for two reasons. Firstly, they allow many party members present to participate in a more active way than simply voting motions and amendments. The importance of such participation should not be underestimated as in moments like these, politics sheds its symbolic mantle and becomes real. Secondly, they allow these same members to sanction party leaders in a very direct way and, equally important, they are another indication of the 'state of play' within the party concerning support for different leaders and tendencies.

These elections also have a latent function concerning individual reputation. Such reputations can be made during an AGM and the direct election to the CNIR at a national level in front of party members can sometimes be seen as a more prestigious political step on the road to recognition than an anonymous regional election.[36] Figure 2.2 shows the voting trends between 1986 and 1992 of elections to the CNIR. This is a different type of vote to that of the motions in that the CNIR is an internal organisation and the election results (re)distribute power within the party. The vote on motions, on the other hand, has a more important external consequence as the victorious motion encapsulates, in theory at least, the political strategy of the organisation for the year to come. The CNIR votes show a fall in support for A. Waechter between 1986 and 1991 with the Voynet tendency taking the lead in 1992. This vote of 1992 was seen by many a political commentator as possibly heralding a new era for environmental politics in France.

It can be seen that *Les Verts* have made serious structural efforts in putting alternative political theory into practice. The changing venue of the AGM, the organisation of the CNIR, the attempts at sexual parity, the mid-term changes in electoral mandates and the limit on the number of individual mandates are all signs of a real wish to implement maximum internal democracy. Some might say this is too much internal democracy in a party which has pretensions of taking power. However, the refusal of the 1990 AGM (Strasbourg) to replace itself with an annual congress open only to regionally-elected delegates (as in most parties) demonstrated the continuing desire of most activists to retain as much direct internal democracy as possible, despite the obstacles it can present to efficiency.

Cultural Practices.[37] Within the environmental movement worldwide, the role of *personal politics* is fundamental. The environment-friendly society, it is believed, will only come about by a mixture of structural and cultural changes. In our survey of 1988, we asked the following question: *What are the environment-*

TABLE 2.2   Environment-Friendly Elements in
             Environmentalists' Lifestyle

Recycling	25 percent
Food	24 percent
Housing/energy	19.5 percent
Transport	14 percent
Others	17.5 percent

Source: Prendiville 1991.

TABLE 2.3 Environmentalists' Consumption Habits

	Every Day	Often	Rarely	Never
Food				
Organic foods:	27.5	36.9	27.5	5.3
Fresh food:				
(non-organic)	31.2	47.6	15.3	1.3
Tinned food:	0.8	23.5	59.9	8.7
Frozen food:	0.8	29.9	45.8	17.1
Recycled paper	24	41.5	28	5.7

Ownership of		*Car ownership*	
electrical appliances		No car:	9.9 (24)
Food mixer:	45.5 (72)	One car:	53.3 (76)
Vacuum cleaner:	89.3 (89)	Two or more:	36.6 (24)
Hair-dryer:	68.4 (78)		
Fruit squeezer:	17.7		
Electric knife:	15.9		
Electric			
toothbrush:	7.2		

Television		*Type of medicine*	
ownership		*chosen*	
No television:	21.9 (7.6)	**Traditional:**	54.6
One television:	67.5	**Homeopathy:**[a]	58.2 (15)
Two televisions or		**Acupuncture:**	15.8
more:	9.9	**Osteopathy:**	13.6
		Others:	14.2

[a] The national average for the use of all types of alternative medicine is 34 percent. Certain national averages are in brackets.

Source: Roche 1990. Figures are percentages.

friendly elements of your lifestyle? e.g. food, vegetarianism, transport, recycling, housing, etc.? (see Table 2.2). These results must, of course, be treated with caution as the definition of what constitutes environment-friendly transport or food are vast. The latter may range from cultivating an organic garden while consuming large amounts of meat to being an active member of an organic food cooperative. It was, nevertheless, revealing to discover that only 9.8 percent of respondents claimed to be vegetarian. Quite obviously, vegetarianism is not an obligatory passport to environmentalism, but within the ongoing debate on animal rights in the Anglo-American world, such a low figure reflects the different nature of environmentalism in Latin countries.

This initial picture of 1988 was modified in 1989 by A. Roche's survey which revealed a population far from the stereotype of the 'brown rice brigade' living by candlelight (see Table 2.3). Within these figures, certain tendencies stand out.

The percentage of families owning two cars or more (36.6 percent) is surprising compared to the national average (24 percent) when one realizes the problem of car pollution. However, as we shall see in Chapter 4, a large number of activists live in small towns which could partly explain this figure.[38] On the other hand, the number of activists without a television (21.9 percent) is higher than the national average (7.6 percent) and this is, surely a cultural choice as the environmentalists are, on the whole, a relatively well-off population. The figures on the use of alternative medicine are less significant as these types of medical practices are now quite widespread and no longer limited to a circle of 'believers'.

The final question in the survey of A. Roche (*Do you think you practise what you preach?*; see Table 2.4) produced somewhat lucid results. In the final analysis, the feeling of most of the environmentalists in the survey that they "more or less" practise what they preach, ties in with this picture of a relatively moderate but coherent population.

TABLE 2.4   Environmentalists: *Do you think you practise what you preach?*

Absolutely	10.3 percent
More or less	67 percent
Not really	21.2 percent
Not at all	0.8 percent

Source: Roche 1990.

Environmental Identity

The environmentalists have spent a long time carving out an independent identity; to the point that the time spent on internal redrawing of environmental blueprints can become overconsuming, as activists at the highest level admit: "Let us stop continually starting from scratch and rethinking the world, it's one of the reasons for our lack of success".[39]

This over-investment in the political word is a reflection both of the French intellectual tradition and, more important, of the necessity of carving out a political niche for an autonomous political movement.[40] How far has it succeeded? Using the political information contained in the aforementioned surveys, we will analyze this identity and, also, consider the exogenous image of the environmentalists formed by endogenous concerns.

The Search for the Grail of Autonomy. One of the problems facing the French environmentalists has resided in the difficulty of fully distinguishing their 'osmosis' from that of the alternative left. Especially during the 1970s, the overlap in beliefs and practices was such that it was sometimes difficult to distinguish an open-minded environmentalist from an open-minded, non-dogmatic eco-socialist. It has proved, however, virtually impossible for the two movements to converge into any form of long-term political structure. The reasons for this are to be found in the disdain of the alternative left towards the environmentalists in the early years (1970s) and, also in the fear of the latter that they would lose their identity by collaborating with the left. The most fundamental reason however stems from a difference in interpretation: the alternative left prefers the institutional left to the right and has proved it in the decisive second round of elections since the advent of the Fifth Republic. The environmentalists believe them to be as bad as each other[41] and since the late 1970s have consistently attempted to distance themselves from the traditional political blocks. They firmly believe that an underlying consensus between the right and the left exists over the major decisions affecting society (e.g. productivism); hence the global rejection of the different political blocks and their accompanying ideologies:

> *Question* (Dominique Souchet): Do you see any difference between François Mitterrand, Jacques Chirac and Raymond Barre? *Reply* (Antoine Waechter, environmental presidential candidate): For the moment, no.[42]

The environmentalists have proved this independence on different occasions by refusing to advise their voters on who to support in the second round play-off of elections and this strategy is quite clear in the aforementioned surveys. In 1984, for example, when activists were asked whether environmental candidates should stand down in favour of a candidate from the right or the left in the second round, an overwhelming majority of 82 percent replied 'no'. In 1989 [1], this figure was 62 percent and in 1989 [2], 61.5 percent of replies were against environmental candidates coming out in favour of a candidate from another party.

Even if this figure has dropped over the years, there still remained in 1989 [1] a two-thirds majority for a line of complete political autonomy, suggesting a "clear perception of the environmental movement as a non-aligned, autonomous political force" (Chafer 1984: 40).

Certainly, environmentalists themselves consider there to be a difference between their political project and that of the alternative left. In answer to this question in 1988, 85.4 percent considered that there was a difference between the two views of social and political action, a figure which was reinforced by the small number of activists who had signed the *Arc-en-Ciel* chart (11.4 percent).[43] One explanation for these figures is to be found in the political trajectory (or absence thereof) of environmentalists (see Table 2.5).

TABLE 2.5   Previous Political Activity of Environmentalists

	1984	1988	1989 [2]
None or no answer	72	85	80
Previous political activity (of which):	28	15	20
-- PS		(1)	(4.5)
-- PC		(4)	(4.5)
-- 'May 1968'	(6)		
-- PSU	(6)	(7)	
-- Extreme-Left	(8.5)	(1)	(6)[a]
-- Anarchist (*Libertaire*)	(2.5)	(1)	
-- RPR			(1)
-- Others	(5)	(1)	(4)
TOTAL	100	100	100

[a] This included the alternative, Trotskyist and Maoist left.

Sources: Chafer 1984; Prendiville 1991; *Sofres* 1989. Figures are percentages.

The relative political 'virginity' of environmentalists is striking. Between 1984 and 1989, around 80 percent of activists had no previous political experience and this figure alone goes some way to explaining the discourse on autonomy. However, when these figures concerning acts are compared with those concerning secondary political sympathies, this position of total independence is qualified (see Table 2.6). The two surveys of 1989 attempted to extract similar information with a question concerning the position of the interviewee on a left-right axis (see Table 2.7).

Two conclusions may be drawn from these figures. Firstly it is patently clear that, over the years, the majority of activists feel themselves to be closer to the parties of the left when asked to choose. More interesting, though, this identification has evolved as the movement has been progressively integrated into the institutions of the Fifth Republic. In 1984, the number of people who identified themselves with the alternative left was almost 50 percent (49.1 percent). In 1988, this figure had dropped to 23.6 percent even if the total percentage for the alternative and extreme left remained relatively high at 37 percent. The decline in

TABLE 2.6   Political Sympathies of Environmentalists

	1984	1988
Extreme-Left	0	13.4
Alternative Left[a]	49.1	23.6
Feminists	0	6.2
PS	11.7	7.3
MRG	1.7	1.7
PC	0	0.6
Others	0	1.7
Total Left	62.5	54.5
CDS	0	1.1
UDF	1.7	0.6
RPR	0.8	0
Extreme-Right	0	1.7
Total Right	2.5	3.4
Regionalists	0	18.5[b]
Others	0	2.8
No reply (or refusal to classify)	35	20.8
TOTAL	100	100

[a] In 1984, the alternative left was the PSU. In 1988, it could have included the PSU and the FGA (*Fédération de la Gauche Alternative*).

[b] This high percentage of regionalist replies is explained by the number of questionnaires sent out in Brittany -- a region with a strong identity -- and the fact that a list of choices was given which included the regionalists.

Sources: Chafer 1984; Prendiville 1991. Figures are percentages

the number of activists in the 1988 survey naming the alternative left (i.e. principally the PSU) as the political family to which they felt closest is undoubtedly due, in large part, to the decline of the PSU as a political party in the 1980s. A significant minority nevertheless continued, at this time, to name the alternative left as the political family to which they felt closest. The results of the 1989 surveys seem significant in this respect, showing a rise in identification with the moderate left and the center, the latter being virtually absent hitherto.[44] In these two surveys, the center reaches 10.6 percent and 17 percent and, taken together, the left and the center-left reach 38.2 percent and 24 percent.

This shift from the extreme-left to the center-left and center

TABLE 2.7   Environmentalists' Position on a Left-Right Axis

	1989 [1]	1989 [2]
1 Extreme-Left	13.3	3
2 Left	19.7	9
3 Center-Left	18.5	15
Total Left	*51.5*	*27*
4 Center	10.6	17
5 Center-Right	2.2	2
6 Right	0.7	0
7 Extreme-Right	0.2	0
Total Right	*3.1*	*2*
No reply	10.7	54
Refusal to classify	24.1	0
TOTAL	100	100

Sources: Roche 1990; *Sofres* 1989. Figures are percentages.

can be explained by three different factors. Firstly, since the presidential elections of 1988, *Arc-en-Ciel* had virtually folded. Secondly, the long struggle for an independent environmental identity was beginning to bear fruit. Thirdly, the then crumbling communist system in Eastern Europe brought with it the crumbling of credibility for any political references which smacked of State communism or socialism. The majority parties on the left (PS, MRG) get off relatively lightly but anything to the left of the PS is totally discredited in the eyes of environmentalists at this time.

The second conclusion has, perhaps, the most long-term political significance and concerns the number of activists who refused to position themselves on a left-right axis. It is always risky to interpret refusals to reply but given the firm environmentalist tendency in favour of political autonomy, these refusals are more significant. Over the five years of survey, there is an average of more than a quarter of activists who refuse to recognize the left-right axis. Is this simply a politically centrist position or, more interestingly, the premiss of a 'turning point' (Capra, 1982) towards a new political culture?

Endogenous Concerns and Exogenous Images

The endogenous concerns of environmental activists can be found in replies to the question on priorities in the 1988 and 1989 surveys. In 1988, activists were asked, *Which areas should Les Verts concentrate on?* (see Table 2.8) and the following year, a similar question was asked (see Table 2.9). Clearly, there is a division amongst environmentalists between those who concentrate on

TABLE 2.8   Priorities for Environmentalists in 1988[a]

Social (Percent)	Natural (Percent)	Others (Percent)
25	47	28[b]

[a] The replies were divided into four answers in order of importance. The first and most significant answer has been presented here. The categories *Social*, *Natural* and *Others* were formed by regrouping the key words: *Social*: Socioeconomic problems, solidarity, anti-racism, democracy, self-management and unemployment. *Natural*: Environment, conservation, recycling, organic farming, animal protection, nuclear, pollution and energy. *Others*: Holism and defense of life.

[b] 21 percent of these respondents replied "holistic". C. Brodhag, ex-spokesperson of *Les Verts*, gave the following definition of holistic: "a global way of thinking about and approaching problems which is contrary to the analytical, reductionist approach that slices reality up into pieces." (Brodhag 1990: 320).

Source: Prendiville 1991.

TABLE 2.9   Priorities for Environmentalists in 1989 [2][a]

Defence of the environment	44 percent
Defend a project of social transformation	39 percent
Help developing countries	22 percent
Fight nuclear power	20 percent
No Reply	34 percent

[a] The respondents had two possible replies. The order was not given with the results.

Source: Sofres 1989.

defence of the natural environment and those who would rather concentrate on the transformation of the social one. A similar division split *Les Verts* in 1986 when two-thirds of party activists lined up behind A. Waechter and the rest supported Y. Cochet. The former defended a strategically political line of total independence from any other party, the latter would not exclude limited contractual agreements with the left.

Two conclusions may be drawn from these figures. Firstly, the image of *Les Verts* which is given to the general public (unaware of internal party debate) is one of people interested in the defence of the natural environment. What is interesting in these results is the confirmation that this image has not been totally fabricated by the media. Secondly, among the category 'Others', 21 percent replied 'holism' indicating that in their opinion, social and natural problems could not be separated. In 1989, 34 percent refused to reply and we can only speculate as to why. Could they also be classed among the 'holists'? Whether they could or not, there remains a sizeable minority which refuses to classify, to dissect or to compartmentalize natural and human problems. Is this more evidence of an environmental paradigm?

Conclusion. In the course of this chapter we have highlighted certain features of the burgeoning environmental political culture. A political culture needs time to ripen and ten years of organized politics may yet be too short a time-span. Moreover, the nature of the national political culture has made life difficult for the environmentalists.

On a structural level, the political system in France is relatively closed which means that any discourse which is not sufficiently integrated into it has little chance of being heard by the general public. The electoral system of the Fifth Republic which divides the country into two opposing camps at each national election reflects this difficulty for minority political groups. The example of the German environmentalists (*Die Grünen*) is often cited to demonstrate how minority groups can live out a healthy political existence in a decentralized federal system.

On a cultural level, the legacy of the French Revolution of 1789 has fostered a form of individualism based on a direct individual identification of the French citizen with the nation State. The consequences of such an individual attachment are twofold. Firstly, citizens often prefer to make demands directly to the State (e.g. President, Administration) instead of through intermediary bodies such as trade unions or associations. Secondly, and somewhat paradoxically, it has rendered him/her directly dependent on the State and, to a large extent, powerless in the face of it and this, in turn, has helped create a form of *unempowerment* (*déresponsabilisation*) which can hinder long-term collective action.

In these circumstances, civil society is weak and cannot constitute the lever against the State the environmentalists would wish for. The anti-nuclear movement's difficulty in scaling the walls of State information on nuclear energy is an example of this. Finally, given the difficulty of channeling social and political protest through intermediary bodies, major social change often takes the form of social explosions. Such explosions, often violent in character, are not an environmental speciality.

Within *Les Verts*, a certain amount of progress has been made in the affirmation of an environmental political culture. The organizational structure reflects the desire for democracy; the CNIR, internal referenda and presidential primaries are each examples of innovations within the French political system. This, at times zealous, desire for internal democracy can produce some unintended consequences and be sometimes unwieldy, but one can hardly criticize a party for attempting to put theory into practice. As for the daily cultural practices of activists, they are fairly much in line with environmental discourse.

With regard to the question of identity, the environmental myth is reflected in the (natural) environmental image which is often attributed to the movement by the media and, indeed, this image coincides with the internal concerns of its majority. During the 1980s, *Les Verts* exploited this natural image very successfully and the sought after autonomy was largely achieved. However, the social dimension of environmentalism is less clear. On the question of the environmentalists' secondary political sympathies, the surveys indicate that they remain on the left even if there has been a shift between 1984 (creation of *Les Verts*) and 1989 (electoral success) from a strong identification with the alternative left to one of identification with the moderate left and centre of French politics.

Will the environmentalists be able to articulate the social and natural facets of environmentalism other than by the written word?[45] Towards the end of the 1980s, the natural image began to pay electoral dividends but the increasing tendency for major parties to use environmental discourse for their own electoral ends may push the environmentalists into fully exploiting the natural and social dimensions of the environmental paradigm.

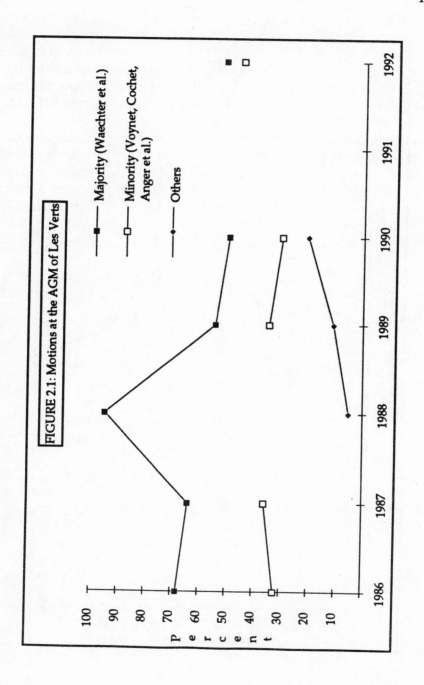

FIGURE 2.1: Motions at the AGM of Les Verts

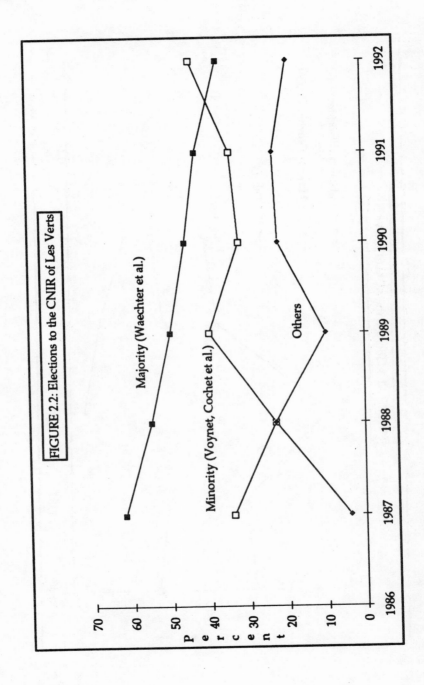

FIGURE 2.2: Elections to the CNIR of Les Verts

Notes

1. A. L. Kroeber and C. Kluckohn, *Culture : A Critical Review of Concepts and Definitions*, New York, Vintage Books (Nd), in Tucker 1973 : 174.

2. The following discussion is indebted to the paper of Patrick 1978. G. Patrick sees, in fact, a fourth interpretation which she terms the "heuristic" approach whose principal exponent is L. W. Pye. We have not considered it because the author considers it "to be devoid of empirical content" (Patrick 1978: 14).

3. (Thomas 1928). Thomas's aphorism was the following: "If men define situations as real, they are real in their consequences".

4. See Fagen 1969, Tucker 1971 ("Communism and Political Culture" in *Newsletter on Comparative Studies of Communism*, LV: 3 May, in Patrick 1978: 17) and Tucker 1973.

5. Linton distinguishes the two forms of culture as follows: "culture as the patterned behavior of man in society and culture as the knowledge, attitudes and values shared by the members of society" (Linton 1945: *The Cultural Background of Personality*, New York. In Tucker 1973: 177).

6. This is not to suggest that the English do not identify with the nation-state as incarnated, for example, in the institution of the Royal family. It is to suggest that the identification of the French citizen is of a different, deeper type.

7. See Viveret and Rosonvallon 1977. The *Jacobins* were the major political force of the French revolution. They considered that a strong central state was a premiss to an egalitarian republic. The *Girondins* (named after the department, *La Gironde*) on the other hand, were worried about the centralization of power in Paris.

8. Napoleon commissioned a legal code (*Code Napoléon*) to unify law for the whole country. It appeared in 1804 and constituted, at that time, a legal revolution by setting down generally applicable rules of law in a clear and concise form, understandable to all. Initially considered an asset, as time went by the lack of flexibility that an insufficiently updated text can engender became apparent. This kind of universal text has also had the effect of reinforcing a certain national uniformity which has denied regional differences.

9. Another example would be that of trade unionism; see Chapter 4.

10. Financially speaking, Mr Benassayag, government spokesperson for Social Innovation and the Social Economy (*délégué général à l'innovation sociale et à l'économie sociale*) was of the opinion that "associations should look for funding other than public subsidies -- at present subsidies make up 80% of

their income" (*Le Monde*, 13 November 1992).

11. The example of various charities, such as the *Restos du Coeur* which distribute free hot meals to the needy in Winter, is the best example here.

12. He made these comments at the 'Forum for the Creation of a New Political Culture' organized by *Arc-en-Ciel* in Paris 19-20 March 1988.

13. In any *département*, the *grands électeurs* are made up of MPs, elected members of the *conseil général* (*conseillers généraux*) and delegates of the municipal council (*délégués des conseils municipaux*). See Potel 1985: 398.

14. This financial situation has improved since their successes in the European elections of 1989.

15. This barrier was abolished for the parliamentary elections of 1993 when, for the first time, each vote cast was reimbursed; see *Libération*, 2 March 1993.

16. In the 1993 legislative elections, two (female) candidates made it into the second round; Dominique Voynet of *Les Verts* and Christine Barthet of *Génération Ecologie*. They were both beaten

17. In municipal elections, the two-round system remains in place and election is by lists. In 1982, the law was modified to introduce an element of proportional representation which had the effect of increasing the number of environmental candidates in the 1983 municipal elections (Chafer 1983: 11-16).

18. In the 1958 Constitution, 15 articles concern the powers of the President, 10 concern those of the Parliament and 4 concern those of government (Potel 1985: 398).

19. This is, in fact, a good example of the "Self-Fulfilling Prophecy" (Merton 1973). Probably the most famous environmental idea transformed into myth is that of Chief Seattle's response to Governor Isaac Stevens when the latter asked the Indian Chief to hand over his land. On the 26th April 1992, the British weekly, *The Independent on Sunday*, revealed that the major part of this speech was written by a Texan script writer in 1971.

20. The 'Gaia' hypothesis has its critics within environmental circles as, if it is pushed to the limits, the idea of a self-regulating organism could dispense with humans altogether. See Beney 1990.

21. This dictionary definition (*Petit Robert*, 1984) sums up the humanist dimension to environmentalism that certain philosophers (see Ferry 1992) find so lacking.

22. Waechter 1986. This desire of A. Waechter is not far from reality as many environmentalists live in small towns as we shall see in Chapter 4.

23. The internal organization of *Les Verts* has given rise to several works: Prendiville 1989 and 1991; Sainteny 1991; Pronier and Le Seigneur 1992. We shall simply concentrate on the original aspects of this organization which are relevant to our discussion.

24. Michels, 1911. There are, of course, 'natural leaders' within *Les Verts*,

but their hold over the party is weakened by these structural efforts.

25. It is possible in France to hold several elected posts at the same time.

26. Rennes, Bordeaux, Strasbourg, Dijon, St Etienne, St Saulve, Paris, Rougiers and Carcassonne.

27. Now that there are two environmental organizations (*Génération Ecologie/Les Verts*) the competition for the presidential candidacy of 1995 will be fierce. There may even be two rival environmental candidates.

28. July S., "Petit glossaire à l'usage des politiques", *Libération*, 21st March 1989. Women make up 53 percent of the French electorate and 5.7 percent of the Parliament; the second lowest percentage in the European Community (e.g. Netherlands: 25.3 percent of MPs are female, Germany: 20.4 percent, Spain: 14.5 percent, Great Britain: 9.1 percent, Italy: 8.1 percent)

29. In 1991 (St Brieuc), there were no individual motions. Instead, there was a joint motion around which revolved debate and division.

30. A. Waechter, Andrée Buchmann and Didier Anger were the three regional councillors elected in 1986

31. IDE = *Initiative Démocratique Ecologiste*; i.e. the contacts made by the outgoing leadership with the alternative left and the associational sector.

32. Daniel Brélaz was the first environmentalist to be elected to a national parliament (Switzerland) in Europe.

33. Parreaux P., "Des Verts... aux Ecologistes", *Supplément au Vert-Contact* N° 6, 1986.

34. 'Fil Vert' was a group which aimed at concentrating its efforts in building a new environmental political culture within the party. By 1992, it had been swamped by the two major tendencies.

35. 'Dynamique' was the title of D. Voynet's motion.

36. It is to be remembered that 75 percent of the CNIR is elected by the regions. The other 25 percent is elected at the AGM.

37. The surveys which provide the quantitative data on activists and voters in this book are the following: 1) Chafer 1984: 132 questionnaires. This survey was carried out in 1983, before the creation of *Les Verts*; 2) Prendiville 1988: 330 questionnaires. Reply rate: 34.5 percent. This survey was carried out in 1987-1988; 3) Roche A. 1990: 4 000 questionnaires. Reply rate: 34 percent. This survey was carried out in 1989 and is herein referred to as 1989 [1]; 4) Sofres 1989: 361 questionnaires. Herein referred to as 1989 [2].

38. It should also be pointed out that several environmentalists drive cars that run on natural gas.

39. Marimot G. (Secretary), "Rapport d'Activité", AGM of *Les Verts*, 1987.

40. This zealous search for autonomy has sometimes led to ideological confusion, as the aforementioned episode with the National Front indicates (see Chapter 1).

41. That position may change since the right has come back into power in

1993.

42. *Source*: France Inter radio, Presidential elections 1988, April. J. Chirac is the leader of the right-wing *Rassemblement pour la République*, R. Barre is an ex-Prime Minister of the centre-right.

43. See Chapter 1 for a discussion of *Arc-en-Ciel*.

44. On environmentalism and political centrism, see Sainteny, G.: "L'écologisme est-il un centrisme?", *Libération* (Collection), March, 1992.

45. K. Whiteside shows that since 1989, "the *Verts'* preoccupations are largely environmental" (Whiteside 1992).

3

Environmental Ideology

What price an environmental ideology? The science of ecology is based on diversity and environmentalism would appear to have followed that lead by spinning a complex ideological web. We shall attempt to unravel it.

Definitions and Functions

The term ideology was first used by the French philosopher Destutt de Tracy (1754-1836) to determine quite simply a science of ideas:

> By ideology he meant a science of ideas, a framework for scientifically analyzing theories and beliefs to discover the truth, eliminate errors and eventually provide the basis of a theory of mental processes. (Slattery 1985: 50)

From an originally scientific, neutral and relatively precise system of explanation, the concept of ideology has progressively adopted a pejorative mantle with vast ramifications. This pejorative connotation is largely due to the interpretations given by K. Marx of the function of ideology in bourgeois society. For Marx, ideology is a form of bourgeois 'smoke-screen' whose aim is to cover up the real nature of class conflict in a capitalist society. In this respect ideology is a tool used by the bourgeoisie to maintain their hold over the working-class by creating the illusion that the capitalist order is the natural order. The class which controls material power in a society also controls spiritual power[1] and the end result of this power is to create a form of 'false consciousness' on the part of the dominated class. Ideology is seen as a production in itself, a production of the dominant class's ideas.

For Marx, therefore, ideology is a part of the general process of alienation by which the workers lose control over the fruits of their labour. This process of conceptual devaluation by Marx explains the fact that the term ideology is now often used to designate other people's belief systems, systems which are held up in derision by their critics whose principal criticism is precisely that they are 'ideological'. It is now often considered to be a conservative phenomenon which holds back the forces of change and, paradoxically, or perhaps coherently, one of the principal criticisms that environmentalists make of Marxism is that of being too ideological.

This then is the pejorative interpretation of ideology but what of its 'neutral' face? Is it possible to use the concept outside the all-inclusive Marxist model in a way that enables us to interpret particular belief systems? Even outside Marxism definitions abound:

a) "A set of definitions of reality legitimating specific vested interests in a society" (Berger and Kellner 1981: 70).

b) "A system of ideas and judgements, generally explicit and organized, which is used to describe, explain, interpret or justify the situation of a group or collectivity and which, principally based on values, offers a precise orientation for historical action" (Rocher 1968: 127).

c) "A set of systematically related ideas and beliefs about the nature of man, society and government which form a framework or theory about how society is or ought to be organized" (Slattery 1985: 50).

d) "Those interpretations of the situation which are not the outcome of concrete experiences but of a kind of distorted knowledge of them which serve to cover up the real situation and work upon the individual like a compulsion" (Mannheim 1943: 89).

Without wishing to choose between or discuss the validity of these few definitions, among many others, certain elements can be extracted. It can be seen for example that ideology is representative of certain groups, that it is descriptive and explanatory, that it is a reflection of values, has a history and contains an element of constraint, and that it has a certain amount of organization. Once these elements are lined up, there comes to the fore an overall impression of homogeneity. Ideology is the result of diverse efforts at theorization and practices over a period of time that have been forged into a relatively coherent and manageable whole. This coherence and manageability is a reflection of its strengths and weaknesses. Its strengths are based on the different functions it can serve in a social movement. It is a powerful force of group cohesion and integration for new members and sympathizers. It provides guidelines and justifications for action, acts as a tool of reference which defines adversaries[2] and equates self-interest with general welfare. Its weaknesses are centered on what could be considered as an advantage; i.e. its comprehensiveness. Such (over) comprehensiveness has produced the *blueprint phenomena* which often enables an ideology to produce answers for unformulated questions, through a process of doctrinal 'predestination'. Such a determinist process is anathema to environmentalists:

> Environmentalism, therefore, has to refuse what is the very strength of doctrines, i.e. not the concrete or exact predictions but the certitudes, 'I have not the courage to present myself as a prophet to my brothers, and I bow to the criticism of not even being able to bring them any consolation. Because that is what they all want, the wildest revolutionaries no less passionately than the bold Pietists' [Freud]. (Brière 1982. No reference was given by the author for the quotation of Freud)

From this initial weakness stem many others. In many ways, an efficient ideology is a static ideology enshrined in sacred texts which, however much they may be up-dated, remain quasi-religious in their import. This kind of faith produces the "distorted knowledge" of K. Mannheim's aforementioned definition which is the inevitable consequence of the simplification of reality. This simplification of reality which transforms *a* reality into *the* reality reveals another important function of ideology; i.e. its capacity to become a reference for millions of people in different circumstances, at different times and in different places. This constitutes a powerful weapon in the constant battle for people's minds and brings the discussion back to the 'Thomas Theorem' (see Chapter 2); i.e. much more important than the supposed veracity of an ideology is the fact that followers use it as a basis for action.

But where does the environmental discourse fit into this discussion? What are the relationships between ideology and the environmentalists?

Ideology and the Environmentalists

The ideology of the environmental movement is an extremely diffuse affair, reaching as it does, from the extreme right to the extreme left of the political spectrum. It is so diffuse that the environmentalists themselves often have considerable problems in presenting a coherent vision of it. This difficulty is however understandable for at least two reasons. Firstly because environmentalism is a relatively recent phenomenon and secondly because it is a movement which claims that the dominant ideologies are part of the problem, seemingly in their content as well as their form. That is to say that, at times, one wonders whether the environmental movement wishes to dispense with the tools of ideology: "we rely on an extraordinary eclectic political and philosophical ancestry. To try to weld this into some easily articulated ideology really would be a waste of time – and would completely miss the point. Ideologies are by definition both reductionist *and* divisive."[3]

There seems little doubt that the activists of *Les Verts* adopt the pejorative interpretation of ideology, using it as an inherent criticism of other people's belief systems. Certain activists speak of "currents of original thought" as opposed to the "ideologies" of the right and left.[4] Others use the term "environmental thought" as opposed to rival political "ideological references" (Waechter 1986). But perhaps a line should be drawn here between the use of ideology as a political tool and as ideological content present in a belief system. In every political movement there is what R. Herbele calls a set of "constitutive ideas" (Herbele 1951: 24) in order to hold people together. These beliefs are not always immediately apparent but it is precisely one of the sociologist's functions to discover what lies behind the facade of social reality; the function that P. Berger calls its "debunking quality" (Berger and Kellner 1981: 12). Through an analysis of texts from 10 AGMs and two international conferences,[5] along with abundant environmental literature and statements, four principal sources of reference have been 'debunked', the order of which is of no importance: Romantic, Authoritarian, Humanist and Utopian. Each of these sources is, or has been at one time, present in environmental discourse and contributes therefore to its set of constitutive ideas.

Romanticism

Perhaps the most widely-held image of environmentalists is that of the 'brown rice brigade' whose principal life-support is carrot juice and who live in candle-lit communes. This image stems from the romantic and conservationist tendencies which have existed within certain sections of the environmental movement, such as during the commune movement of the 1970s. From Jean-Jacques Rousseau complaining that trees are made to stand to attention in French gardens: "Does nature constantly use a set square or a ruler? Are they scared that we may still recognize it despite efforts to deform it?" (Simonnet 1979: 100) through to an advert for environmental holidays in 1988: "With local people, from wayside resting places to farms, outings on foot, horse or on skis, moving with shepherds in the footsteps of J. Giono, savouring wholesome local food, with your head in the stars and your feet in a field of ammonites",[6] the theme of a romanticized clean life away from the insalubrious 'nature' of town life is one which is at the heart of the environmental collective consciousness. Indeed, it could be seen as the starting block of the environmental movement via the different conservationist groups that accompanied industrialization in the country (Vadrot 1978).

Coupled to this outer cleanliness is an inner one that is considered by many to be as, if not more, important. 'Fundamental change comes from within' could be the slogan that underpins a philosophical and religious tradition as incarnated in the debate between idealism and materialism. Over the centuries, materialism, no doubt, won this debate and the 'deep' side of the environmental movement sees as one of its tasks the (re)incorporation of idealism and more especially spirituality into human action.[7] The excesses of this approach are to be found in the belief that social change can be brought about by an aggregate of individual consciousness raising based on the power of intuition: "Each of us has within himself a spark of creative power, of universal energy which can change the inner and outer world. This power, which everybody has, is the result of thought processes, not just intellectual ones, but those which come from deep thought, from thought of the heart."[8]

Authoritarianism

The authoritarian undertones within environmental discourse have raised their heads on different occasions:

> -- I await the arrival of a world government which can oppress populations in order to bring down populations and reduce pollution as well as to change desires and behavior by psychological manipulation;
> -- insidiously a code of licence and amorality is being created, backed up by social security payments and benefits of various kinds (...) this freedom which gives way to irresponsible licence and this permissiveness which is encouraged by social security reimbursements for activities such as dangerous driving, abortion and dangerous sports, only pushes individuals into passionate and perverse excesses [e.g. drugs, homosexuality, adultery, abandoning of children, incest]. (Pronier and Le Seigneur 1992: 191 and 194)

The first quote is from Jean Fréchaut and the second from Dr Gillard, the tireless defender of alternative medicine at the AGMs of *Les Verts*. Both have been members of *Les Verts* and were active in the 'fundamentalist' tendency which appeared in 1986 and 1990.[9]

The doubts as to the real 'nature' of environmentalism are linked to its attachment to things of the land. History has its precedents and this fear was brutally summed up by A. Grosser: "It is no accident if environmentalism took off in Germany where nature — *die natur* — is perceived very differently. The forest — *der wald* — is a strong symbol (...). In France this conservative tradition has less of a history, except perhaps for that which stretches from Vichy to Jacques Tati in *'Mon Oncle'*: 'Long live that which is non-industrial, agricultural; the farmer, the tree and the plough'." [10] Such a reactionary picture of environmentalism has tainted its appeal for many a prospective activist and voter even if the party political nature of certain attacks has often been visible.

Pursuing this line of reasoning further, and from a purely theoretical point of view, there is a more worrying train of thought present in environmentalism which could lead down a more potentially dangerous path. This concerns the use and extension of the organic analogy to social structures. The environmental paradigm bases itself on an organic, systemic view of the social and natural world which fundamentally opposes Cartesian dualism. Human beings are no longer viewed as 'masters and possessor of nature' but as an integral part of it. Such a view often projects itself through organic metaphors which, in themselves, are as ancient as Shakespeare when Menenius Agrippa compared the Senators of Rome to the 'belly' in *Corialanus*. In the field of Sociology, H. Spencer (1820-1903) was the first to apply the organic analogy to social structure and in doing so laid the basis for the Functionalist school of thought. However, the potential dangers of leaning on organic, biological analogies are that they take over. That is to say, they may lead to a form of 'biological imperialism' by which the social order is governed by biological principles. What is in question at this point is the concept of the self-regulating systems that environmental writings often refer to. This concept, based on systemic and cybernetics theory, assimilates a future environment-friendly society to that of an open system, similar to that of a living organism within which individual units (e.g. cells/individuals/towns) exist in a state of mutual interdependence. Mutual interdependence means that each unit is dependent for its survival on the whole but retains a measure of autonomy, allowing it to evolve as it sees fit. The system as a whole is, consequently, self-regulating via a process of input/output and positive and negative feedback in much the same way as a cybernetic machine. This, at least, is the open-ended, optimistic interpretation of systems-cybernetic theory as applied to the social structure. A more pessimistic, restrictive version would be the kind of 'vision' outlined by C. Barrier-Lynn:

> Is not the image of a self-regulating system destined to favour a form of status quo? Would not cybernetic policies simply be giving power to the scientists? And what is to prove that they would not yield to the temptation of an enlightened despotism? (Barrier-Lynn 1975:191)

The possibility of extracting two radically different visions of the future from the same body of thought illustrates the ambiguous nature of the systemic approach when applied to the social structure. There is the risk, in the same way as Auguste Comte had somewhat hegemonic pretensions for *his* 'science of society' (i.e. sociology), that environmentalism may also have delusions of grandeur; i.e. to become the total, global science to which all others are subjugated.

The temptation to extrapolate from the sciences into the social and political worlds is ever present in the environmental movement and is understandable when one considers the high proportion of scientists who have taken part in its history. It is reasonable to suggest that the majority of activists are now aware of this danger.[11]

Humanism

At a time when certain French intellectuals are beginning to have doubts as to the real nature of environmentalism,[12] the debate on environmental humanism has taken on added importance. It can be traced back to two sources: Ivan Illich and Emmanuel Mounier. The former is a world-wide reference in environmental literature and a direct influence whereas the latter is a more indirect influence on French environmentalism via the Personalist school of thought he founded in the 1930s.

I. Illich. Without Illich, environmentalism would not be environmentalism. He has been an inspiration for the French environmental elite and writers over the past twenty years, from B. Lalonde to S. Moscovici and from A. Gorz to R. Dumont. He is not as well-known today amongst activists but his work on conviviality and the theory of thresholds remains a linchpin of environmental theory.

Conviviality has become a very fashionable term in recent years. 'Sociable and lively' is one dictionary definition and in computer language it is synonymous with 'user-friendly'. In the vocabulary of Illich however, 'conviviality' has a more precise meaning concerning social organization and human relationships:

> As an alternative to technocratic disaster, I propose the vision of a convivial society. A convivial society would be the result of social arrangements that guarantee for each member the most ample and free access to the tools of the community and limit this freedom only in favour of another member's equal freedom. (Illich 1973: 25)

Such a vision brings together three different strands of environmental humanism. Firstly, the political liberalism reminiscent of humanists such as John Locke and John Stuart Mill. Secondly, the struggle against technocracy. Technocrats, in environmental vocabulary are those people who control, to a large extent, the destiny of society. The capitalists are deemed to have lost a lot of their control to this new class which controls knowledge and technology and uses it, all too often in the minds of environmentalists, at the expense of human beings' welfare.

The third strand is that visible in Illich's notion of the 'tools'[13] and its accompanying concept of autonomy. A convivial society is one in which people can control its tools: "Defence of conviviality is possible only if undertaken by the people with tools they control" (Illich 1973: 125). Autonomy is a linked notion in that convivial, human-scale tools allow individuals the autonomy necessary to participate in the running of society.

As a corollary to his ideas on conviviality, Illich formulated the 'Two Watersheds Theory'. In it he describes the process by which an institution can pass through two watersheds; the first one being that of efficiency and conviviality, the second one of inefficiency and harm. In Illich's opinion, most industrial tools have passed, or are passing these two watersheds and rendering, in the process, individuals increasingly dependent on them. One example of this process is that of transport: "it has taken almost a century to pass from an era served by motorized vehicles to the era in which society has been reduced to virtual enslavement to the car" (Illich 1973: 20).

The rehumanization of society is synonymous, therefore, with convivial reconstruction.

Personalism. The second source of French environmental humanism is that of Personalism. This was a school of thought whose principal exponent was E. Mounier[14] (1905-1950), co-founder of the famous revue *Esprit* in 1932. Mounier's aim was to create a movement based on a doctrine of social and moral humanism which would herald a new civilization. Such a form of revolutionary humanism, in Mounier's opinion, was necessary in the face of a rampant materialism (East and West) that had the effect of producing either an individualistic form of social Darwinism or a face-less, bureaucratic collectivism. This relationship of Personalism and environmentalism has been highlighted by D. Allan Michaud (1979) and we will mention three striking instances.

Mounier was dismayed by the incapacity of the institutionalized left to imagine anything other than the utilitarian, consumerist tools of capitalism as a model for a future Socialist society. In this respect, the environmentalists have taken up, virtually verbatim, ideas which have a fifty year-old history:

> the greatest trial of the 20th century will no doubt be to avoid the dictatorship of the technocrats who, be they right-wing or left-wing, forget man under the organization. (Mounier 1949: 115)

Prophetic words indeed which reflected the Personalists' concern over the direction which Western industrial society had taken through a form of social mechanization. This social mechanization was held responsible by Mounier for the depersonalization taking place in Western society which led to a form of individualistic atomization. It was not a question of refusing technological progress but rather of opposing its excesses and this directly reflects another tenet of the environmental paradigm; i.e. the watershed theory mentioned above.

The second parallel between environmentalism and Personalism concerns the concept of autonomy. The vocabulary may have changed over the years but for both schools of thought, this concept means the articulation of individuality and solidarity. For Mounier, this articulation was called the "Unity of Persons" (Mounier 1949: 42) and concerned the need for individual identity *and* collective unity in society. For the environmentalists of today, the concept is pushed further by considering the individual unit — be it an individual, a community or a region — to be a free entity within a superior whole of which it is an integral and necessary part. Seen in this light, autonomy is clearly distinguishable from individualism; the former aims to cement the social bond, the latter does more to weaken it.[15]

"The nature of the whole is always different from the mere sum of its parts" (Capra 1982: 287) sums up this idea of individual and collective autonomy within a free association of responsible persons. Autonomy as a Personalist and environmental concept is translated politically and strategically in similar fashion by independence from the power blocks. "Neither left nor right, nor in the centre, nor 'elsewhere', the *Movement for Political Ecology* intends to be in front" (MEP 2 1980) was already a popular environmental slogan in the early 1980s and for Mounier this principle also constituted a way forward: "At least in the beginning, independence from established parties and groups is necessary to fully measure new perspectives" (Mounier 1949: 112). The suggestion that an independent political line is only necessary at the outset of a movement's existence is highly interesting, given the ongoing debate within environmental circles concerning political alliances.

A final parallel that may be drawn between the Personalist movement of the 1930s and the environmentalists of today is in the field of sociopolitical priorities. The political and social themes put forward by Mounier in his defence of Personalism strongly resemble environmental concerns and three examples bear this out. Firstly, Mounier was a fervent feminist:

> it is true that our social world is made by men for men and that humanity has not massively delved into the depths of the feminine being. (Mounier 1949: 118)

Secondly, he considered that federalism was an answer to many of the world's problems in a similar way to environmentalists' support for political decentralization. Finally, he took a firm stand, as do environmentalists, against ethnocentrism and racism: "equality amongst persons excludes, obviously, any form of racism and xenophobia (...) there is not *one* culture next to which all other activity is ignorant but as many diverse cultures as there are activities" (Mounier 1949: 119, 124).

Personalism, therefore, is very much a philosophical forerunner to the environmental movement and both environmentalists and Personalists recognize as much (Allan Michaud 1979: 1013-1015).

Utopianism

Diversity being the environmentalist rule, this fourth branch of their ideological tree has three seperate twigs: anarchist, millenarian and futurist.

Anarchist. There is, outside the dominant centralist tradition in socialism, a decentralist, self-managing current embodied in the 19th century utopian socialist movement which is not a million miles away from environmentalism. Themes such as a desire for a human scale economy based on political and economic decentralization; for labour-intensive cooperative-type production as opposed to a capital-intensive, monopolistic system; for work which is socially useful in content and which leads to a more equitable distribution of wealth; all these are themes which anarchists, democratic socialists and environmentalists would adhere to, be they from Europe or from the USA. This historical and philosophical link between anarchism, socialism and environmentalism has been referred to at various points during the short life-span of the French environmental movement. Whether it is emphasized or not depends on the period in question. During the 1970s, one of the principal environmental papers (*Le Gueule Ouverte*) boasted of its anarchism by hoping for: "The disappearance of parties, of the vote, of the delegation of power and of hierarchies and, therefore, of the State"[16] and one famous environmental theorist (Denis de

Rougement) once described himself as being "completely Bakunian" (Allan Michaud 1979: 850). Others, such as D. Simonnet and P. Lebreton, consider that the environmentalists have given a new lease of life to ideas which had gone out of fashion:

-- The old federalist and anarchist cause, tortured by history, has found a new lease of life with environmentalism. (Simonnet 1979: 83);
-- The most obvious analogy is to see the environmentalists take up, one century later, what was usually called the benevolent utopias of the first socialists. (P. Lebreton in Allan Michaud 1979: 851)

This anarchist tradition should not be underestimated as it explains certain attitudes and practices within the environmental movement. With regard to attitudes, for example, it can be seen as the reason for the scorn environmentalists pour over the communist movement which is a reflection of the traditional enmity between anarchists and communists. Equally, it explains why secondary political sympathies amongst environmentalists have traditionally been closer to the anarchists than to the Trotskyist or Maoist movements on the extreme-left. Similarly, it is no surprise to see that the ex-leader of the French 1968 student movement, D. Cohn-Bendit, subsequently decided to join the German greens.

At least three environmental practices can be explained by reference to this anarchist tradition. Firstly, the favorite environmental sport of 'head chopping' could be seen against a background of reticence towards leaders in general. One northern green light, Guy Hascoët (*Les Verts*) explained this tendency in the following terms: "Having left the 'mad head choppers' loose within the environmental movement, all the leaders' heads which stuck out have been chopped off."[17] Secondly, the direct democracy-type atmosphere of *Les Verts*' AGMs, even if they are now more organized, is also a measure of this tradition. Finally, this tradition is visible in the greater political power of the regions within the governing body of *Les Verts* (i.e. the CNIR).

The environmentalists of the 1980s and early 1990s have made much less reference to the anarchist and democratic socialist ideals of their predecessors given their overwhelming desire to forge their own political identity and political culture.

One potential problem however with such a 'start from scratch' strategy is the creation of a form of historical amnesia.[18]

Millenarian. One of the consequences of this 'start from scratch' tendency is the millenarian phenomenon which has always been latent within the environmental movement. Millenarianism is a term which has been applied to those movements, principally religious, that await ultimate, collective and total salvation with the coming of a saviour.[19] The classic example of such movements are the Amerindian movements of the 19th century or the Melanesian Cargo Cults in the early part of this century. Both were movements of an ecstatic, hysterical nature that mobilized support around the myth of a historically pre-determined new age. This is not to say that the environmentalists have within their ranks, ecstatic or hysterical elements, nor that it awaits a saviour. It is, however, to suggest that there are instances which date back to its early 'catastrophic' period of a 'new age dawning' vision of social reality that periodically appear. D. Simonnet picked up on this tendency quite early: "Despite their quasi-scientific appearance, the alarmist warnings often sink into prophesies and sometimes mysticism. The initial environmental discourse was an example of this type of millenarian anxiety" (Simonnet 1979: 98).[20]

Futurist. Amidst the wealth of environmental literature there is a strand of thought lying just beneath the surface that might be called futurist in that it conceives of a better future by means of technology:

> Environmentalism does not, therefore, refuse technical progress as has often been said. On the contrary, the most radical strand, represented by Murray Bookchin, would be rather over-optimistic in suggesting that technological possibilities are unlimited and that the most sophisticated techniques, highly efficient products stemming from a meeting of biology and computer science, could be used to lighten the workload of man. (Simonnet 1979: 72)

The question is, will this society be one which will be technologically 'liberating' and ecologically acceptable or will it be a perfected form of social and political domination? Because therein lies the crux of the hope in the new technologies; that they will be conducive to the kind of convivial society which environmentalists aspire to. This hope is visible in two sectors: communication and energy.

Many people would say that within the confines of the 'information society', communications are becoming a premiss to effective democracy. At the same time, IT (information technology) is a multinational product, much like any other commodity,[21] bought and sold through telephones and computers. In France, the development of the videotext has opened up possibilities of individual and collective communication that inspire some environmentalists: "[we should] work towards a more direct democracy with methods using less delegation such as the referendum by popular initiative (RIP). Within this context, Les Verts suggest studying the possibilities of using the télématique."[22] Such possibilities leave others cold: "The RIP is a fair idea because it is democratic. However, it is meaningless unless the vote is the result of a real and serious debate. Otherwise, it becomes a fabulous means of manipulation and Le Pen[23] has fully understood this with regard to immigrants and the death penalty. I am very surprised to see that certain Verts want to study the possibilities of using videotext in this area. Where would the debate be?"[24] One recent example of this environmental attraction to new technologies is to be found in the voting system at the AGMs since November 1992. At the AGM of Chambéry and the emergency AGM of June 1993, votes were computerized and virtually instantaneously flashed up on the screen. Given the ease with which votes could be taken, the principal consequence of this high-tech democracy was that activists spent almost as much time voting as they did debating.

In fact, the question as to the advantages of modern technology in promoting a more participatory society is a very ambiguous one. The French sociologist, Edgar Morin, is of the opinion that a rise in the standard of living can be a reflection of a lowering in the quality of life: "the multiplication of means of communication can be tied to the impoverishment of personal communication" (Morin, Kern 1993: 97).

The second sector is that of energy. We have seen that nuclear power combines all that environmentalists believe should be socially, politically and ecologically excluded from future society. Hence the proposals and faith in alternative energies and, in particular, solar energy as a way out of the energy maze. The adage 'small is beautiful' reflects the belief that for solar energy, or any other source of power, to be democratically controllable it must be sufficiently small. As an example of what can be achieved in this domain, Californian experiences are often held up as showpieces of modern environmental and technological inventiveness. The question remains: how will cleaner energy sources, indispensable as they certainly are, transform social relationships and cultural lifestyles? The panacea of the sun has not convinced the German environmentalist, D. Cohn-Bendit:

> I am beginning to get really fed up with debates which try to show how the same amount of energy could be produced by solar energy. I think that the American Defence Department has shut a whole part of the anti-nuclear movement up by saying: "It is true, perhaps we should ask ourselves whether we couldn't supply our American military bases in the desert with electricity from solar energy." So, we would have atomic missiles on one side and a solar energy military base on the other. Consequently, solar energy in itself isn't a reply to anything and moreover, the largest investments are now being made by multinationals which have understood that the solar energy future holds out enormous possibilities. (Castoriadis and Cohn-Bendit 1981: 54-55)

This futurist source of French environmentalism illustrates the type of opposition to be found within its discourse. On the one hand, it is suggested that a technique may be liberating in itself and, on the other, only if social relationships allow it to be.

The utopian tradition in the environmental movement is, therefore, one which raises its head periodically under different forms. Since the outset of environmentalism, the anarchist form is the most important and traces can still be seen in *Les Verts*. It was, however, more visible during the 1970s when extra-institutional political activity was at its strongest. During the more recent period (1980 - 1993), environmentalists have spent a lot more time and energy in carving out their own niche within the political system. In these circumstances, utopianism has faded somewhat, to be replaced by the humanist branch against a background of philosophical attacks on the potential dangers of environmentalism (Ferry 1992), and the rise of the extreme-right in the country.

Conclusion. Ideological content is always present in a social movement in some form. If the term ideology hurts too much, it could be called a belief system. The belief system of the environmentalists is one which activists would like to consider as systemic; i.e. bringing together diverse but complementary strands of thought into a coherent whole. We believe that, for the moment, it is more syncretic in that the strands of thought in question seem quite contradictory at times. Such a syncretic belief system has its advantages in that people of apparently different social and political horizons can come together under the environmental banner. It can also have its disadvantages when the contradictions in perspective between these different beliefs appear in the full light of day. Its limits have perhaps been reached as the efforts in forging a new, alternative political culture could indicate. That is to say that the ideological eclecticism we have unearthed is perhaps a luxury which it can no longer afford and that from now on greater conceptual clarity will be needed if it is to confirm its wish to remain 'in front'. The conference organized in January 1992[25] is, no doubt, a sign of this trend.

Perhaps a better description of environmental ideology at this stage is that of *axiology*; i.e. a system of values which leaves the future open and which represents more of a kind of moral code than what we are accustomed to calling ideology: "environmental awareness also contributes, in its own way, to enforcing the idea of indispensable and common, minimal rules, a sort of 'oecumenical morality'" (Lambert 1990: 95). Indeed the environmentalists themselves prefer the term 'values' when promoting their beliefs. The four which are most often cited are those of *democracy, solidarity, autonomy* and *responsibility*. A common set of values could be the first step in the creation of a new, less dogmatic form of environmental ideology.

Notes

1. In this respect Marxism is a materialist philosophy as opposed to an idealistic one. Life is not the incarnation of ideas, ideas are rather "the language of real life" (Cot and Mounier 1974: 121).

2. A. Touraine, for example, considered that the main adversary of the ecologists was technocracy (Touraine 1980).

3. Porritt 1984: 200. The quotation is English but the import is, we believe, general.

4. Carré M., Perrigueux M., Masquelier G., Massip B&G: "Quel chien dans un jeu de quilles?" (Motion), AGM of *Les Verts*, Paris, 1986. In *Supplément au Vert-Contact* N°6, 1986.

5. AGMs: Besançon 1983; Dijon 1984; Paris 1986, 1987, 1988; Marseille 1989; Strasbourg 1990; Saint-Brieuc 1991; Chambéry 1992. *Assises Nationales de l'Ecologie Politique*: Paris 26-27 September 1992. European Ecologist Congresses: Dover (GB) 1985; Paris 1989. AGMs of the Breton Ecologist Federation (*Fédération Ecologiste Bretonne*): Lorient (*Morbihan*) 5 May 1985; Lorient 26 October 1986; Loudéac (*Côtes d'Armor*) 26 September 1987; Lorient 23 October 1988; L'Ile Berder (*Morbihan*) 20-21 October 1990; Rennes (*Ille-et-Vilaine*) 24-25 October 1992. *Assises de l'Ecologie en Bretagne*: L'Ile Berder 19-20 September 1992. Local meetings of *Rennes-Verte*: 1983 to 1994.

6. Extract taken from the publicity of *Association Plein Air Nature* in the presentation brochure of *Salon Vivre et Travailler Autrement*, 19-27 March, 1988, Paris. This exhibition was the second of its kind, wishing to publicize the French 'alternative' under its many different guises (e.g. health foods, naturism, alternative work practices) and more, therefore, a manifestation of the horizontal axis of environmentalism. The following extract sums up this strand of the wider environmental movement: "l'APRI (*Association pour la Protection contre les Rayonnements Ionisants*) has given birth to quite a number of sometimes old associations which were created for a specific reason; e.g. vaccinations, naturism, organic agriculture, hygiene by plants, etc., groups preoccupied with a more 'natural' lifestyle. If some of their members appear somewhat conservative, irrational or sectarian, there is, however, no doubt that the vast majority of these associations were the forerunners of the environmental movement" (*Collectif Ecologiste* 1977: 19). J. Giono (1895-1970) was a French writer well-known for his reverence of nature and country life.

7. The word *spirituality* is used here in the sense of a doctrine which maintains that the mind constitutes an independent and superior reality to matter. As such spirituality is not simply the reflection of a formal religion but of values which transcend material reality. On the importance of spirituality in worldwide environmental discourse, see Capra 1982 and Porritt 1984.

8. "Transformez Votre Vie par la Pensée Positive" in *Evolution: Fédéralisme-Ecologie-Mondialisme*, review distributed at the AGM of *Les Verts*, Paris, November 1987. Another example of the importance given to personal development in social change is shown in the following extract from a motion of the 1986 AGM of *Les Verts*: "Personal development is a capital feature of social evolution... Pacifism is built on an inner peace" (Lecuyer 1986).

9. We can still remember the presentation by E. Fournier of the motion "For a fundamentalist tendency in *Les Verts*" at the AGM of 1988. He defended "fundamental values" and spoke of "physical and moral health". He invoked the "light of the Party" and ended by crying out "Long live environmentalism, long live conviviality". The hall, in hilarious uproar, ironically replied "And long live France".

10. Grosser A.: "Faut-il avoir peur de l'écologie?" in "Tout sur les écologistes", *Libération* (Collection), March 1992, p.65. A. Grosser is a professor at the *Institut d'Etudes Politiques* in Paris. Vichy was the headquarters of the collaborationist government of Pétain during the Second World War. *'Mon Oncle'* is a film (J. Tati 1958) about the clash between old and new worlds. See also Alphandéry, Bitoun and Dupont 1991.

11. The well-known German environmentalist, D. Cohn-Bendit, gave the following warning on just this danger: "an authoritarian environment-friendly society is quite conceivable. This possibility stems from the ambivalent relationship between the environmental and anti-nuclear movement and the social institution of science. Often warnings are given and solutions proposed on the basis of knowledge which those who are struggling do not possess. The way forward is sometimes hailed as being under the banner of a supposedly neutral, rational and universal knowledge which is valid for the whole of society" (Castoriadis and Cohn-Bendit 1981: 15).

12. See Ferry 1992.

13. The term 'tool' covers the common sense idea (e.g. hammer) or the wider notion of a system and/or organization (e.g. education, political, economic system).

14. The philosopher C. Renouvier (1815-1903) was the first to use the term.

15. A. Lipietz uses the term in another way to describe the individual's right to control his actions [*"voir le bout de ses actes"*] (Lipietz 1993: 18).

16. *La Gueule Ouverte*, N°80, 19th November 1975.

17. Hascoët G., "Je Dis Oui" (Motion), AGM of *Les Verts*, Paris, 1986 in *Supplément au Vert-Contact* N°6, 1986. At the time, certain activists were of the opinion that the leadership of A. Waechter was a reflection of the rank and file's rejection of political charisma.

18. At the inaugural meeting of *Arc-en-Ciel* (Paris, 18 January 1987), G. Cohn-Bendit, brother of Daniel, was the first to point out this "ahistoric" tendency within *Les Verts*.

19. In the revelations of St John and in Jewish apocalyptic literature the saviour was Christ. For the Melanesian 'Cargo Cults', he came in the form of a boat full of European goods (see Wilson 1973: 50-52).

20. More recently, activists were informed that "tomorrow's society will be environmental or not at all.". See Bassot E. (among other signatures), "Ni droite, ni gauche: Verts" (Motion), AGM of *Les Verts*, Marseille, 1989 in *La Tribune des Verts*, N°3, 28 October-3 November 1989.

21. In 1986, IBM controlled 80% of the world's mainframe computer market (Weston 1986: 67).

22. Cochet Y., "Construire" (Motion), AGM of *Les Verts*, Paris, 1986.

23. Extreme-right leader of the *Front National*.

24. Fournier A., "Réflexions" (Contribution), AGM of *Les Verts*, Paris, 1986 in *Supplément au Vert-Contact* N°6, 1986.

25. Bordeaux : *De l'identité des Verts*, 9-10 January 1993.

4

Typology and Social Base of French Environmentalism

This final chapter will look at French environmentalists themselves. Who are they and where do they come from? Is it possible to draw a clear profile of the typical activist and can we talk in terms of an environmental social base?

The Social Base

In 1951, Rudolph Herbele declared that social movements are "as a rule closely bound to certain classes and opposed by others" (Herbele 1951: 14). Such a statement poses two questions. Firstly, does the environmental movement represent a particular social class struggling for power and recognition in advanced capitalist society? Or, secondly, if it is the reflection of more general concern, how far does it reach into the different social classes?

Do the environmentalists represent a particular social class? The (manual) working class was seen as the natural social base for the socialist movement. Is there any equivalent for the environmentalists and, if so, which is the class in question? The orthodox Marxist analysis suggests that green politics is "an attempt by a specific social group to come to terms with its incorporation into the social relationships imposed by capitalism" (Weston 1986: 27) and that environmentalists suffer from their "narrow middle class base" (Weston 1986: 29). *Les Verts*, on the other hand, see themselves as a vehicle taking on board all those groups working for sociopolitical and economic alternatives:

Be it in the organization of social or citizen pressure groups, or the search for social and economic alternatives, Les Verts, while respecting everyone's independence, put themselves forward as a meeting place for apparently different forms of militant action.[1]

It is at this point that the debate on the importance of post-materialism, or post-industrialism, which stimulated theorists at the beginning of the 1970s may be encountered.[2] This concept is often linked to the growth of the environmental movement (Lowe and Rudig 1986) and postulates a society based on services rather than production, in which the control of knowledge and information is the key to political and economic power.[3] The blue collar classes are gradually replaced by the white collar ones as a technocratic elite replaces the owner classes traditionally associated with capitalism. This general theory on macro-social change has been seen as a causal factor in the rise of environmental movements in the West. The theory holds that the environmentalists represent an emerging, post-materialist class whose basic material needs have been satisfied and who are now beginning to concentrate on "higher order needs" (Lowe and Rudig 1986: 515). They may be beginning to "pull up the draw-bridge"[4] by concentrating on 'quality of life' concerns while the lower classes try to satisfy basic material needs. This division between materialists and post-materialists is seen as replacing the old divide between capitalists and workers in a different form:

However, it is not a question of a 'new class struggle' along the lines of 'proletarians versus capitalists' but rather of a *mosaic of social groups and citizens* (e.g consumers, transport users, regionalists and feminists) struggling against certain groups called technocrats who, more than the political class, have the final power of decision in numerous sectors (e.g. energy, transport, urban and regional development). (Cochet 1984 [a])

This bursting asunder of social conflict is seen as being at the heart of a fundamental shift in Western values which now place qualitative demands on a par, if not above, quantitative ones (Inglehart 1971 and 1977). Are the environmentalists the political representatives of post-materialist theories?

The hypothesis is enticing in its simplicity but a definitive answer to such a question is, of course, impossible. That the environmental movement has evolved within a society undergoing fundamental social and economic change is self-evident. That it is, in part, a result of these changes (e.g. pollution, population explosion) would also seem to be the case and is reminiscent of Neil Smelser's insistence on structural change (Smelser 1962) as a factor in the appearance of a social movement. That the generation of the 1960s, which is at the heart of the environmental elite, was brought up amidst the myth (if not always the reality) of the *Affluent Society* (Galbraith 1961), and that the opposition movement of that decade which culminated in May 1968 was as much a protest over an alienating economic and social system as one in favour of a greater share of the national cake would also seem to be true. However, there are two problems with this hypothesis.

Firstly, the Marxist interpretation of class consciousness considers that a level of class consciousness is indispensable to its ripening. This process of maturity is coupled with the identification of the worker to his work. In contemporary society however, as Gorz points out, there is an increasing distance of the worker from his work:

> It is no longer a question of the worker freeing himself through his work or of mastering his work (...) It is now more a question of freeing himself from work by refusing the nature, content, necessity and form. (Gorz 1980: 103)

In this context of weakening individual identification with the world of work, the conscious formation of a post-materialist class encounters difficulties.

The second problem is more theoretical and concerns the inherent ambiguity of the term itself which may be viewed in a positive or negative light. On the negative side, there is the underlying supposition that, if the post-materialists are 'pulling up the draw-bridge' of materialism, they are acting purely in their own individual interests which brings the discussion around to A. Oberschall's 'resource management theory' (Oberschall 1973). Inspired by M. Olson's 'rational theory approach', Oberschall considers individual interest to be the major motivation in social movement activity. However, this type of approach does not appear to fully correspond to the environmental movement for two reasons.

Firstly, and while the importance of self-interest in social movement activity cannot be discounted, to consider self-interest as the overwhelming motivation in collective behaviour is to deny the importance of beliefs and ideals which are highly present in environmentalism, albeit in a syncretic manner. Secondly, the question remains concerning analyses of gain and political control; who stands to gain from a successful environmental movement? While it is true that many social movements claim to act in the general interest, the environmental movement claims to differ from mainstream politics by aspiring to modify both the content *and* the form of contemporary society (i.e. how the wealth is created as well as its distribution).

In a more positive light, post-materialists are seen as those people who have seen the flaws in industrial society and who are beginning to contest the rationale of it:

> The ideological shift characteristic of post-materialists is not found among all environmentalists, some of whom are quite comfortable with the dominant values of the system. The overlap is rather between post-materialism and those recently developing elements of the environmental movement that have begun to articulate a critique of the techno-scientific rationale of industrial society. (Watts and Wandesforde-Smith 1981)

"Those recently developing elements" are, in fact, those environmentalists who articulate *social environmentalism* with *natural environmentalism*, that is, the defence of the natural environment coupled to analysis and critique of social relations and power-sharing in modern economies. Given the ambiguity of the term 'post-materialist', the question as to whether the environmentalists are a political expression of it remains open.

Concerning the extent to which environmentalism reaches into different social classes, the best response is a quantitative one. This will be done by presenting a comparative study of four surveys carried out between 1984 and 1989[5] with a view to drawing a sociological profile of the environmental activist and sympathizer.[6]

A Typology of Environmentalists

In a social movement, the activists are the people who play the key role in defining the movement's policies, strategies and campaign priorities. In this section, a typology of environmentalists will be presented with a view to outlining their social and professional status, their age and level of religious and social commitment. In order to shed more light on any particularities, comparative surveys of environmental and socialist voters at the European elections of 1989 and of Socialist Party activists (PS: *Parti Socialiste*)[7] will also be presented. The PS was chosen as a comparison because the surveys carried out on the secondary political sympathies of the environmentalists clearly demonstrate that the closest school of thought is that of the left (see Chapter 2).

Sexual Parity?

Despite wishes to the contrary, *Les Verts* remains a men's party (see Table 4.1). In France, as elsewhere in the Western world, men are more politically active and, therefore, the male majority is no surprise. However, within the context of environmental discourse, these figures are revealing. The French environmentalists have given less emphasis to feminism and eco-feminism than, for example, their German counterparts.[8] This difference in emphasis is reflected in these figures.

TABLE 4.1   Gender Divide between Environmentalists, Socialists and their Voters

	Activists				Voters	
	Verts 1988	Verts 1989 [1]	Verts 1989 [2]	PS 1990	Verts 1989	PS 1990
Men	74.6	72.6	70	81	49	52
Women	25.4	27.4	27	19	51	48
No Reply			3			
TOTAL	100	100	100	100	100	100

Sources: Sofres 1989; Prendiville 1991; Roche 1990. Figures are percentages.

When compared with the PS figures, however, *Les Verts* appear relatively feminized.

An Ageing Movement?

The age group structure of *Les Verts* did not alter radically between 1984 and 1989 as Table 4.2 illustrates. In 1984, the largest age group was that of the 31 - 40 years (41 percent) and this supported the claim that the environmental movement was principally that of the generation of 1968. Three years later however, the situation was virtually identical with the same age group in the majority (39 percent). In fact, there is a continual

TABLE 4.2   Age Groups of Environmentalists, Socialists and their Voters

	Activists					*Voters*	
	Environ[a] 1984	Verts 1988	Verts 1989 [1]	Verts 1989 [2]	PS 1990	Verts 1989	PS 1989
Under 20			0.9				
18 - 24				10	4	15	8
18 - 30	31	21.9					
20 - 30			22.6				
25 - 34				34	14	31	20
31 - 40	41	39.5	39				
35 - 49				38	56	29	30
41 - 50	16	16.7	17.7				
50 - 64				13	21	17	23
51 - 60	6	10.5	9.6				
Over 60	6	9.6	9.4				
Over 65				3	4	8	19
No Reply		1.8	0.8	2	1		
TOTAL	100	100	100	100	100	100	100

[a] *Environ* refers to environmental activists as this survey was published in 1984 but carried out in 1983 when *Les Verts* did not yet exist.

Sources: Chafer 1984; *Sofres* 1989; Roche 1990; Prendiville 1991. Figures are percentages.

TABLE 4.3   Membership Figures of *Les Verts:* 1984 - 1989

	1984	1985	1986	1987	1988	1989
Ongoing members	513	628	718	808	914	1,301
Returned ex-members	0	0	55	111	131	174
New members	559	536	443	376	874	2,849
Percentage (new members)	52	46	36	29	45.6	65.9
TOTAL	1,072	1,164	1,216	1,295	1,919	4,324[a]

[a] Since the boom year of the last municipal elections (1989), this percentage of new members has stabilised around 30 percent. In 1993 the total membership stood at 5,684 with 27 percent of new arrivals.

Source: Document of *Les Verts*, AGM Marseilles, 1989. Our percentages.

turnover in membership within *Les Verts*, an observation which is corroborated by an internal party document of 1989 (see Table 4.3).

There was a major influx of activists into the party after the municipal election successes of 1989. The survey of 1989 [1] suggested that the members who joined *Les Verts* in the period between 1988 - 1989 were relatively younger than their predecessors: 29 percent of them were under 30 years old, as opposed to 17 percent of the members who joined between 1984 and 1987. The results of the 1989 elections also suggested that there continues to be a reservoir of support for environmentalists among younger voters.[9] The ability, or otherwise, of *Les Verts* to capitalize on this support and turn it into active commitment will be an important factor affecting the party's development.

When compared to the PS figures, two points stand out. Firstly, 56 percent of socialist activists in this survey were between 35 - 49 years old, as compared with 38 percent of environmentalists in 1989 [2]. Secondly, the age difference between socialist activists and their voters is greater than that between environmental activists and their voters. In 1989, 46 percent of *Les Verts'* voters were under 34 years old which corresponds with the 44 percent of their activists within this age group. On the other hand, the survey of the PS revealed that only 18 percent of their activists were under 34 years old with 28 percent of voters being of the same age. Quite obviously, the party then in power had a more established political personnel.

One final point concerning the environmental ideology and strategy is reflected in these figures. The constant turnover in party personnel facilitates the radicalism of the 'neither left nor right' position as well as the historical amnesia we revealed in the environmental belief system. The reasons for this are twofold. Firstly, When there is such a turnover, internal political socialisation is an annual process and always revolves around around the notion of political autonomy. Secondly, such waves of new recruits can push the party as a whole into constantly rediscovering the world through green eyes.

Religion

Religious practices have declined quite drastically over the last thirty years. In 1965, there were 40,994 Catholic priests, in 1975 this figure had dropped to 36,014 and in 1984, 30,000 priests took their religious vows. At the same time, the level of religious identification has also dropped. In 1986, 86 percent of the people surveyed declared they were Catholic and in 1984, this figure stood at 79 percent, 53 percent of whom did not practise. Of the practising Catholics, 37 percent went to church every Sunday, 22 percent once a month, 22 percent on major religious occasions (e.g. Easter, Xmas) and 16 percent for certain ceremonies (e.g. baptisms, weddings) (Potel 1985: 546).

As can be seen from Table 4.4, the environmentalists are not a particularly religious population. Indeed the reverse would be surprising given the anarchist leanings we have noted and the national context of declining religious influence.

The comparison of religious practices amongst socialists and environmentalists is particularly interesting. The number of practising Catholics amongst socialist activists is small (7 percent) and this is a reflection of the political and religious divide over the question of public and private education in the country. This divide has often followed party political lines and the association of lay schooling to the socialist movement has been automatic since Jules Ferry (1832 - 1893) instigated lay educational reforms at the end of the nineteenth century. Perhaps a continuing

TABLE 4.4 Religious Practices amongst Environmentalists, Socialists and their Voters

	Activists				Voters	
	Verts 1988	Verts 1989 (1)	Verts 1989 [2]	PS 1990	Verts 1989	PS 1989
Catholics	61.3 [a]	45.5	34	42	77	79
Practising	(10.5)		(22)	(7)	(21)	(23)
Non-practising	(50.8)		(12)	(35)	(56)	(56)
Other religions	8.9	9.4	9	6	3	2
Practising	(3.5)					
Non-practising	(5.4)					
No Religion	28	43.9	54	50	20	19
No Reply	1.8	1.2	3	2		
TOTAL	100	100	100	100	100	100

[a] The higher percentage of Catholics in the 1988 survey is due to a large number of answers from the Celtic region of Brittany, a traditional bastion of the Catholic church.

Sources: *Sofres* 1989., Roche 1990, Prendiville 1991. Figures are percentages.

Personalist influence explains the higher number of practising Catholics within the ranks of the environmentalists (1989 [2])?

A Social Elite?

In our opening discussion on the environmental social base, we evoked the post-materialist hypothesis. This begs the question concerning the social status of activists which we shall now consider under the sub-headings of profession, education and income.

Profession.[10]It is first of all clear that a large proportion of environmentalists have jobs (88 percent in 1984, 72.8 percent in 1988, 72.6 percent in 1989 [1], 80 percent in 1989 [2]; see Table 4.5). In contemporary France, this is worthy of note and means that the most valid comparisons are with the working population (see Table 4.6). Secondly, a large number work in the tertiary sector, with the professional and educational professions being especially well-represented. It is equally clear that few of them come from either the farming community or the manual working

TABLE 4.5   Professions of Environmentalists, Socialists and their Voters

	Activists					Voters	
	Environ 1984	Verts 1988	Verts 1989 [1][a]	Verts 1989 [2]	PS 1990	Verts 1989	PS 1989
*Agriculture	2.3	1.8	3.2	2	1	2	2
*Self-Employed/ Shopkeepers/ Small Business Owners	3.8	6.1	5	5	2	4	2
*Professional/ Education (secondary and higher)	43.2	32.5	33.6	35	51	8	5
*Intermediate/ Education (primary)	25.8	21	25.3	22	26	21	16
*Employees	9.1	9.6	10.2	9	4	18	16
*Manual Working Class	3.8	1.8	3	4	1	10	13
*Not in Work	12	20.2		13	11	37	46
(students)	(3)	(5.3)					
(unemployed)	(3.8)	(2.6)					
(retired)	(3.8)	(10.5)					
(others)	(1.4)	(1.8)					
*Other professions			0.4	3			
*No Reply		7	19.3	7	4		
TOTAL	100	100	100	100	100	100	100

[a] In this survey of 1989, the percentages of the categories are of the *working* population (all the other surveys are of the *total* population). The total results of this survey were as follows: Working population: 72.6 percent, Unemployed: 4.8 percent, Not in Work: 22.6 percent (retired: 10.7 percent, at home: 4.7 percent, student: 7.2 percent).

Sources: Chafer 1984; *Sofres* 1989; Prendiville 1991; Roche 1990. Figures are percentages.

TABLE 4.6 Socioprofessional Categories in France

	Total Population	Working Population
*Agriculture	2.7	6.3
*Self-Employed/ Shopkeepers/ Small Business Owners	3.4	7.8
*Professional/Education (secondary and higher)	3.5	8
*Intermediate/Education (primary)	7.3	16.9
*Employees	11.5	26.6
*Manual Working Class	14.3	32.9
*Retired	13.7	
*Not in Work	43.6	
*Unemployed never having worked		1.5
TOTAL	100	100

Source: INSEE 1990: *Tableaux de l'économie française*, Paris. Figures are percentages.

class. The same is true of the socialists.

The low number of environmentalists working in the agricultural sector can be partly explained by their criticisms of the pollution caused by contemporary farming methods. It is also, however, confirmation of the essentially urban nature of environmentalism. The low percentage of employees is, on the other hand, a reflection of the nature of this class itself which is overwhelmingly female.[11] It is, however, the figures of the Professional/Education sector which demonstrate the widest gap between the survey results and the national averages. In 1989 [1], 33.6 percent of environmentalists and 51 percent of PS activists fell into this sector, compared with a national average of 8 percent (working population). Part of the explanation is to be found, again, in the nature of the category itself which is as male dominated as the environmental (and socialist) activists appear to be; in 1985, only 25.9 percent of the Professional/Education was made up of women. A corollary explanation concerns the number of people working in education. In 1984, 31.8 percent of environmentalists worked in the education sector and in 1988 this figure reached 35 percent.

The importance of the tertiary sector in general and the educated social categories in particular are the most salient features of this professional breakdown. With regard to environmentalists this can be explained by the wider evolution of society and its own specific aims, the latter of which go some way to explaining the relative lack of manual workers within its ranks.

In 1962, more than 20 percent of the working population worked on the land, the Intermediary classes and the Self-Employed/Shopkeepers/Small Business Owners classes were of the same size and the Professional/Education classes represented less than 5 percent (Seys 1987: 37). In 1990, 6.3 percent worked on the land, the Intermediary classes were twice as large as the Self-Employed/Shopkeepers/Small Business Owners and the Professional/Education classes had almost doubled (8 percent). The national and international tertiary sector had increased dramatically and it is quite natural that this general trend is reflected in the environmental professional breakdown of today.

However, the disparity between the national and the environmental breakdown remains sizeable and this is more a reflection of environmentalism's distinctive concerns. Initially, environmentalism came into the public eye amidst a wave of concern in the early 1970s over the fate of planet earth and has been associated with the defence of the *natural* environment ever since (despite attempts by activists to modify this stereotyped image). The principal cause of the pollution that is deteriorating the natural environment is, it is claimed, the Western productivist system which is held up as a model to the rest of the world and which has been built up on manufacturing industry over the last century. The manual working class remains (just) the major professional class in French society with 32.9 percent of the working population in 1990 and it is this class which is the most associated with the manufacturing sector of the productivist society that environmentalists so criticize. It is, therefore, not surprising that few members of it are to be found within the environmental ranks (i.e. approximately 3 percent).

TABLE 4.7 Education levels of Environmentalists, Socialists and their Voters

| | Activists | | | | Voters | |
	Verts 1988	Verts 1989 [1]	Verts 1989 [2]	PS 1990	Verts 1989	PS 1989
Primary	5.3		3	1	22	39
Secondary	27.2	37.7	19	17	23	18
Technical or Commercial[a]			12	11	21	20
University	64.9	59.1	60	64	34	23
No Reply	2.6	3.2	6	7		
TOTAL	100	100	100	100	100	100

[a] This category is included in the *Secondary* line of the 1988 and 1989 [1] environmental activists' surveys.

Sources: Sofres 1989; Prendiville 1991; Roche 1990. Figures are percentages.

Education. The figures of Table 4.7 are strong confirmation of an intellectual elite, both amongst socialists and environmentalists. For the latter, they are also a reflection of the importance of the teaching professions previously illustrated.[12]

Income. A further element in this discussion on the social status of environmentalists is family income. Is it above average and how does it compare with that of environmental voters and the PS figures?

The environmentalists remain a financially well-off population although they could not be classed as rich (see Table 4.8). In 1988, 19.3 percent earned less than 7,500 Francs per month. In 1989 [1] and 1989 [2], this figure was 31.1 percent and 26 percent respectively which indicates a slight drop in overall income as the total population increased. It is, however, within the middle income bracket (7,500 - 15,000) that the highest percentages are to be found with 35.9 percent in 1988, 42.1 percent in 1989 [1] and 45 percent in 1989 [2].

This picture of a relatively well-off financial situation is reinforced with a comparison of the national monthly *salaried* income. In 1988, the national monthly income stood at 8,400 Francs (INSEE, 1989) and in the three surveys of 1988, 1989 [1]

TABLE 4.8   Monthly Income of Environmentalists

	Activists				*Voters*	
	Verts 1988	Verts 1989 [1]	Verts 1989 [2]	PS 1990	Verts 1989	PS 1989
Under 3 000 Fr[a]	3.5	6	4		6	5
3 000 - 5 000 Fr	5.3	9.1	8	1	8	14
5 000 - 7 500 Fr	10.5	16	14	4	19	20
7 500 - 10 000 Fr	7.9	17.1	19	10	19	20
10 000 - 15 000 Fr	28	25	26	18	22	20
15 000 - 20 000 Fr	12.3	16.4	16	22	9	11
Over 20 000 Fr	5.3	7.9	10	43	9	4
NO REPLY	27.2	2.5	3	2	8	6
TOTAL	100	100	100	100	100	100

[a] Fr = French Francs.

Sources: *Sofres* 1989; Roche 1990; Prendiville 1991. Figures are percentages.

and 1989 [2], 45.6 percent, 49.3 percent and 52 percent of environmentalists respectively earned above 10,000 Francs.

When the figures of environmentalists' earnings are compared with those of the PS, the former almost seem to be in a position of 'relative poverty'. In 1990, 43 percent of the socialists earned above 20,000 Francs, 65 percent above 15,000 Francs and 83 percent above 10,000 Francs. Another interesting comparison is with the voters' earnings. In 1988, 1989 [1] and 1989 [2], 5.3 percent, 7.9 percent and 10 percent of environmentalists respectively earned above 20,000 Francs while 9 percent of their voters were in the same wage-earning bracket. On the other hand, 43 percent of the socialists earned above 20,000 Francs while a mere 4 percent of their voters reached this sum. The party then in power was made up of a certain elite.

By way of a conclusion to this discussion on the social status of the environmentalists it could be said that, whether or not they are the political manifestation of a new social class thrown up by the post-materialist or "programmed society" (Touraine 1980 [b]: 6), the term 'social elite' seems slightly excessive, especially when compared to the figures from the PS. What these figures do reveal however, is that the environmentalists have few inroads into certain major sectors of French society (e.g manual working

TABLE 4.9   Place of Residence (i.e. size of town) of
Environmentalists and Socialists

	Verts 1989 [1]	Verts 1989 [2]	PS 1990
Under 2,000 inh[a]		20	12
Under 2,500 inh	31.6		
2,000 - 10,000 inh		17	20
2,500 - 10,000 inh	16.4		
10,000 - 20,000 inh		9	12
10,000 - 50,000 inh	21.1		
20,000 - 50,000 inh		16	20
50,000 - 100,000 inh	9.3	10	10
Over 100,000 inh	21.6	26	25
NO REPLY		2	1
TOTAL	100	100	100

[a] inh = inhabitants

Sources: *Sofres* 1989; Roche 1990. Figures are percentages.

class, farming) while being heavily represented in others (e.g. intellectual, tertiary). This absence is perhaps not surprising and, indeed, could be seen as a normal state of affairs for a movement which aspires to gain power in the 21st century. It does, however, present a problem for those in the environmental movement whose main concern is gaining a "cultural majority" (A. Waechter), similar to the ideological hegemony Gramsci considered as a necessary premiss to the socialist revolution.

Housing. The housing situation of environmentalists highlights two points. Firstly, the rate of home ownership and, secondly, the size of the town or village of residence.

The 1989 [1] survey was the only one of the four to have produced detailed figures of the accommodation structure. There is, therefore, no comparison to be made. It is, however, worthy of note that the rate of home ownership amongst those polled was 37.1 percent which is above the national average of 26 percent. With regard to the type of housing, only 7 percent of those polled lived in low-priced council housing (HLM) as opposed to 14.4 percent of the French population (INSEE 1989).

Within the context of an environmental discourse which tends to glorify the village way of life, the figures on the environmentalists' place of residence are interesting (see Table 4.9). Inside *Les Verts*, A. Waechter came to power in 1986 by evoking this image of small town life: "the *commune*, and especially the small village *commune*, is the foundation of the society we aspire to. To neglect it would be a serious mistake" (Waechter 1986).

The principal feature of these figures concerns the number of activists living outside large urban conurbations. The discourse on the importance of the small *commune* and its desired way of life has some significance when it is considered that almost half the people surveyed in 1989 [1] (48 percent) live in a town of under 10,000 inhabitants and 31.6 percent in one of under 2,500 inhabitants. The opposition between the greater conviviality and social integration of small town life and the urban anonymity of the city present in environmental discourse is highlighted by these figures. Small town life forms a part of the daily experience of activists even if the electoral support is principally urban (Boy, 1989). The figures of the PS would seem to confirm this environmentalist predilection for small town life, given that only 12 percent of the PS sample live in a village of under 2,000 inhabitants.

Social Commitment. One final feature of this activist profile which is of interest is what may be called the level of social commitment; i.e. the rate of unionization and membership in associations.

In France, membership of a trade union is nowadays tantamount to a political statement. The situation is different in other European countries, be they in the north or the south, Protestant or Catholic (see Table 4.10).

The rate of unionization among environmentalists is higher than the national average (Table 4.11[13]). Such an observation has to be qualified as we have already seen that there is also a large percentage of teachers which is, traditionally, a heavily unionized sector in France. This rate of unionization is, nevertheless, worthy of note as it tempers the picture of well-off egotistic environmentalists, 'pulling up the drawbridge' of prosperity

TABLE 4.10 Rate of Unionization in Europe

Country	Percent
Denmark	80
Belgium	75
Portugal	60
Eire	59
Luxemburg	49
ex-FRG	43
Great Britain	43
Italy	39
Greece	35
Netherlands	30
Spain	17
France	10

Source: Le Monde, 5 December 1989.

TABLE 4.11 Trade Union Membership of Environmentalists and Socialists

	Environmentalists 1984	Verts 1988	Verts 1989 [1]	PS 1990
Unionized (of which)	31	37.7	24.9	60
-- CFDT	(24.4)	(16.6)	(10.8)	
-- SGEN		(4.4)	(2.4)	
-- SNES		(2.7)	(2.5)	
-- FEN	(5)	(4.4)		
-- SNI			(2)	
-- Others	(1.6)	(9.6)	(7.2)	
No Reply	69	62.3	75.1	40
TOTAL	100	100	100	100

Sources: Chafer 1984; Sofres 1990; Roche 1990; Prendiville 1991. Figures are percentages.

behind them. This rate is, however, in decline since the creation of *Les Verts* (1984: 31 percent, 1989 [1]: 24.9) which may reflect the individualist, enterprise culture discourse so prevalent in France during the 1980s.

Of those who are unionized, the largest contingent belongs to the independent left-wing trade union, the CFDT. Before its change of direction (i.e. *recentrage*[14]), this trade union used to be considered the most sympathetic to environmental issues, largely because of the central role it played in the anti-nuclear movement in the 1970s as well as in other movements of the day (e.g. feminist, regionalist, etc.). It was in this context that A. Touraine saw the anti-nuclear movement, and the environmental movement which accompanied it, as a prophetic movement which would "be a part of the major shift from an industrial to a post-industrial society" (Touraine 1980 [a]: 333 - 335). For this shift to be a success, Touraine suggested that the best strategy for the movement to adopt would be to ally itself to those groups, such as the CFDT, which were fighting the same adversary. In the burgeoning post-industrial society this was no longer the capitalist class of factory owners but rather the technocratic elite which is in a position to determine the collective destiny of society. The CFDT was seen as a natural partner of the environmental movement because: "it is a trade union of the modern sectors of the economy in which operators and technicians can take limited action for better professional status but can also lead a new social movement by preventing (technocratic) structures from controlling knowledge and by joining up with users' struggles against these structures."[15]

Since the anti-nuclear activity of the 1970s, the CFDT and the environmentalists have gone their separate ways for two reasons, other than the general decline in union membership. Firstly, the strategy of *recentrage* meant that the CFDT deliberately refrained from participating in social movement activity during the 1980s, considering that its association with different causes during the 1970s was perhaps detrimental to its image as a trade union whose main task is to defend workers' rights.[16] Secondly, the transformation of the environmental movement into a political party in 1984 distanced it from the CFDT, given the strong links between the CFDT and the party in power during the 1980s (i.e the PS). Correspondingly, the PS survey shows a far higher percentage of trade union membership.

The level of social commitment is also measurable in the rates of membership of various associations (see Table 4.12). It is apparent that the majority of environmentalists carry out their social commitment within associations as opposed to trade unions. This highlights the importance of this sector, in activists' eyes, as a platform for environmentalism; that is, one which is not confined to the workplace. Moreover, this illustrates the view amongst many environmentalists that there has been a shift in emphasis of social conflict in contemporary Western society which is reminiscent of A. Gorz's comments on the weakening of identification with work and also ties up with Alberto Melucci's comments on the complexity of modern society (Melucci 1989). Such a weakening of traditional professional ties coupled with an increasingly complex social system has, many activists believe, 'burst social conflict asunder' and created a 'mosaic' of social struggles opposing citizen groups to technocrats. In this context,

TABLE 4.12   Association Membership and Typology for Environmentalists and Socialists

	Verts 1988	*Verts* 1989 [1]	*Verts* 1989 [2]	PS 1990
Membership:				
Member of at least one association	89.5	74.2		
Not a member	10.5	25.8		
TOTAL	100	100		
Type of associations[a]				
Environmental		67.3	62	11
Social or civic		33.6	49	59
Other or unspecified		9.7		

[a] The figures here do not add up to 100 percent as several answers were possible.

Sources: Sofres 1989 and 1990; Roche 1990; Prendiville 1991. Figures are percentages.

action within associations is a perfect platform for social movement activity.

With regard to environmental ideology and axiology, this taste for associationist militancy is a reflection of two things. Firstly, it is a reflection of the anarchist utopianism we saw in the environmental belief system. Environmentalists consider that this type of extra-institutional, social movement type political activity is an indispensable complement to more traditional party politics. Secondly, the world of the associations (*vie associative*) is the perfect setting for the environmentalists' value of autonomy. It is in this kind of setting that the individual has a better view of the consequences of his acts and, also, a certain amount of control over these same acts. That is to say, that working in associations gives the individual a greater sense of responsibility than working in the more bureaucratic surroundings of the political party or trade union and this reinforces a feeling of individual empowerment.

Concerning the type of association preferred, it is interesting to note the difference between the environmentalist and socialist emphases. In similar proportions, the environmentalists prefer environmental associations (1989 [1]: 67.3 percent, 1989 [2]: 62 percent) while the socialists prefer social or civic associations (59 percent). The difference between the two political families is quite clear at this point.

What Do the Activists Think?

As a final point, it is interesting to note the self-conceptions of activists in this domain. What do they think of this notion of a social base? "A political movement cannot exist without a social base" was the reply of A. Uguen (*Verts*, Quimper) but most of our interviewees[17] were less categorical, giving rise to three different conceptions.

Firstly, the vast majority of our interviewees were of the opinion that the real or potential social base of environmentalism could not be limited to one or more definite classes. In the minds of activists, the overwhelming impression was one of diversity. However, this diversity was interpreted in a positive and negative way. On a positive note, the idea of one class or social group as the principal support for environmentalism was seen as a handicap in that environmental problems were, or should be, the concern of all the social classes. On the other hand, and more negatively, this diversity was also seen as proof of the vagueness of environmentalism which was a reflection of the lack of a clear political project. That is, as it stood, it was able to attract individuals from all the social classes who were concerned about environmental damage but that this force of attraction would not necessarily extend to a common political project and was, therefore, limited in scope.

Secondly, those interviewees who were prepared to go further suggested that the "enlightened middle classes" was all that could be seen as a potential social base of support. In using this expression, J-Y Le Touze[18] summed up the opinion of many interviewees who believed that environmentalism was as an outlet for concern for those social groups which worked in the tertiary sector and which had a certain social and educational standing. This links up to the previous comments on the preponderance of intellectuals within the environmental movement.

Finally, the only group to see a clear (potential) social base was that of the organic food activists. The organic producers in particular suggested that *they* were the practising social base of environmentalism but that the environmental activists, up to the present, had virtually ignored them.

Conclusion. By way of an answer to the initial question on the existence of an environmental social base, in terms of professional categories it is the massive presence in the Professional/Education category which is the most remarkable feature of these surveys (the PS has an even higher proportion within this category indicating a similar intellectual activist base). The importance of this neutral, sociological observation should however be tempered as it is relative to the aims of the environmental movement, which are themselves relative to the different conceptions of environmentalism. Is the environmental movement involved in a struggle for power in the political sphere or is it, rather, more concerned with the dissemination of alternative beliefs and practices. Or is it a mixture of the two?

If the strategy is principally electoral and political, the increasing importance of the media reduces the importance of reaching into the different social classes, in recruitment terms at least. If, however, the aim is cultural, as well as electoral and political, the efforts may have to be increased in order to make effective social and cultural contact across the professional categories.

More fundamentally, the discussion on the existence of an environmental social base poses a more general problem as to what constitutes a social base for any social movement in contemporary society. Western society may not yet be the "programmed society" that A. Touraine spoke of at the end of the 1970s. It is, however, certainly the "complex society" which Melucci speaks of (Melucci 1989) and which is characterized by our difficulty to fully explain the complex problems confronting us. Such a society, if social movements still exist as Melucci himself wonders, needs new forms of social analysis. Class relationships may still be important but analysis which remains based on class conflict alone is insufficient to understand the nature of conflict in modern society, as the ex-*Vert* F. de Beaulieu pointed out: "the social base of the environmental movement is not based on classes, or on the relationship to production but on the relationship to life. We now need to reason in different terms; e.g. the rate of nitrates, time spent on transport and the raising of children, etc.". The experience of the anti-nuclear movement is ample proof of the incapacity of orthodox class analysis to explain collective action in contemporary society. If economic and professional relationships remain, quite obviously, major explicative factors in social movement activity, their relative importance has declined in the face of other social and cultural factors. The rise of environmentalism is as much the result of changing personal and collective perceptions of the natural environment as it is of economic and/or professional relationships. The search for profit may well remain a major cause of pollution but the most well-intentioned technocrat can cause as much environmental damage as a 'profit-hungry capitalist' in the eyes of many environmentalists.

Notes

1. Bousseau C., Buchmann A., Cambot G., Devoucoux B., Gueydon Y., Hascoët G., Marimot G., Richard-Molard C., Vidal J.-L., Waechter A.: "Motion d'orientation", AGM of *Les Verts*, Paris, 1988. In *Vert-Contact* N° 82 bis, 1988.

2. See Bell 1973; Touraine 1969; Toffler 1981 [a].

3. Toffler puts forward the following definition of post-industrialism: "a society in which the economy is largely based on service, the professional and technical classes dominate, theoretical knowledge is central, intellectual technology -- systems analysis, model building, and the like -- is highly developed, and technology is, at least potentially, capable of self-sustaining growth" (Toffler 1981 [a]: 443).

4. Chafer 1984: 38. T. Chafer uses this expression as an allusion to the argument of M. Tozzi (Tozzi 1982) that the environmental movement could be seen as trying to prevent the working classes from obtaining the benefits they themselves enjoyed from the polluting, consumer society.

5. The four surveys are those mentioned in Chapter 2; i.e. Chafer 1984; Prendiville 1991; Roche. 1990; *Sofres* 1989.

6. Amongst environmentalists, the notion of 'sympathizer' is more important than elsewhere given the extreme suspicion with which many potential activists consider party politics. This means that they often refuse to enter the arena of traditional politics while participating in wider social movement activity. It is for this reason that we have included readers of the weekly bulletin of *Les Verts* (*Vert-Contact*) and ex-party members of *Les Verts* in this category of activist-sympathizers.

7. The survey of the Socialist Party activists was carried out by the *Sofres* for the daily newspaper, *Le Monde*, at the conference in Rennes (Ille et Vilaine, 16 March 1990. Total number of replies: 1,021 [including 722 delegates, 103 *parlementaires*, 62 members of the *Comité Directeur* and other "declared activists"]). It is not our intention to analyze this survey. It is of interest only in so far as it was carried out in similar circumstances (and by the same organization) to the other *Sofres* survey of November 1989 (1989 [2]) concerning the environmentalists. The figures concerning the environmentalist and socialist electors are other elements of comparison. They concern the European elections of 1989 and caution must be taken in extrapolating tendencies given that these elections are still considered less important than national elections. No survey details (e.g. number of voters surveyed) were given with the voters' figures.

8. In the aftermath of the German State elections of 1986, the environmentalist parliamentary 'fraction' was composed of 25 women and 19 men.

9. On environmentalist voters, see Boy 1981 and 1989.

10. The social classes referred to are those of the French statistical institute: INSEE. It must be pointed out that the category *Agriculture* does not encompass the same professional field as in the English-speaking world. More often than not, the persons placed in this category are what are termed *paysans* i.e. small farmers. The *Professional/Education* classes include secondary school teachers. The *Intermediary* groups are those skilled social categories which include primary school teachers, social workers, the clergy, civil servants (*fonctionnaires*), technicians, foremen, etc. and the 'new' professions linked to health, education and the social services such as youth group leaders, speech therapists and psychotherapists. The *Employees* include such professions as office personnel (public and private), police and military, shop assistants, etc.

11. In 1985, 74% of employees were female and we have seen that 75% of environmentalists are male.

12. A supplementary aspect of this concentration of intellectuals is highlighted by G. Sainteny when he singles out the high proportion of environmental leaders with a scientific background as opposed to a law or social sciences one, which is the case with the left or right elites. This could herald the formation of a new type of elite within the Fifth French Republic. See Sainteny 1990.

13. The 1989 [2] survey on environmental activists asked one question concerning trade union sympathies (*Give a mark -- between 1 and 10 -- to the trade union you feel closest to*), the answers to which were the following; CGT: 2 percent, CFDT: 4.7 percent, FO: 2.8 percent, FEN: 3 percent, FNSEA: 1.3, percent CNPF: 1 percent.

14. *Recentrage* was the name given to the CFDT strategy adopted in May 1979 by the congress in Brest (Finistère). This strategy consisted in targeting the activity of the trade union on strictly union issues as opposed to the wider political activity of the 1970s.

15. Touraine 1980: 320. This is reminiscent of the previous discussion on post-materialism even if there was never any official alliance between the environmentalists and the CFDT.

16. An interview with a full-time representative of the CFDT (A. Dorso: 19 April 1990) confirmed this. Given the present unemployment crisis, whether a trade union should limit itself to this role is, today, a debatable point.

17. The following comments are based on a series of 103 interviews carried out in Brittany between 1980 and 1990 in the following populations: *Verts* (25 interviews), organic food producers (17), third world activists (11), environmentalists (18), alternative left activists (9), regionalists (10), others -- e.g. university professors (13). See Prendiville 1991.

18. Regionalist municipal councillor in Lorient (Morbihan).

Conclusion

This study has traced the nebulous environmental movement of the 1970s to the two institutionalized political organisations of the 1990s. Does this mean that the environmental 'social movement' no longer exists? What is a social movement in 1993? Does the term retain any meaning in an age (i.e. Western age) of social atomization and social change of supersonic speed? Has society become too complex to study globally? The definitions of what constitutes a social movement abound and *the* homogeneous, Marxist conception of a social movement is light years away from the environmental conception of heterogeneity and diversity. The environmentalists do, nevertheless, have a sociopolitical project but the question remains: how far has it penetrated into civil and political society?

Environmental ideology is difficult to pin down. "So much the better" would be the activists' reply who repudiate the term ideology. Ideology for them is synonymous with Marxism which they consider to be rigid, dogmatic and too simplistic for our complex societies. This notwithstanding, ideological content is always present in political activity and environmentalism is no exception. However, its mixture of idealism and pragmatism gives it a particular flavor. Be it scientific or political, environmentalism is based on the notion of *diversity* and the different sources we revealed (romantic, authoritarian, humanist and utopian) could be seen as the logical outcome of this diversity. It is certainly the case that environmentalists want to avoid the creation of a belief system that provides answers to unformulated questions but, without going that far, we are left with an unanswered question: is the opposition between the social and natural branches of environmentalism simply a reflection of this diversity or, rather, a reflection of an underdeveloped belief system? The proposals for a more equitable society based on the respect and defence of the natural environment remain sufficiently vague to attract the support of wide sections of the (voting) public. With the first successes of 1989, the limits of this ideological vacuum have perhaps been reached, assuming that environmentalism does not simply wish to become an effective environmental pressure group.

The study of national and environmental political culture gave us an insight into both the obstacles confronting French environmentalism and into its true 'nature'. The national political culture is not conducive to autonomous sociopolitical movements. The centralizing, Jacobin tradition and the individual unempowerment it engenders place the French citizen in a position of dependence which renders long term collective action difficult. As a result, civil society is relatively weak and this slightly vicious circle poses a problem for a movement which sees the associationist sector as its sociopolitical springboard. On top of this, the relatively closed political system (e.g. electoral system) coupled to the individualist discourse of the 1980s made life difficult for French environmentalism up to the end of this decade.

As for the environmental political culture itself, it helped us understand certain facets of environmental analysis. The somewhat naturalist image that *Les Verts* retain in the public consciousness is a reflection both of environmental symbolism and activists' concerns. The environmental myth, based on 'thinking globally and acting locally', explains why environmentalists were the first to talk in terms of *planetary individual existence*. The political and cultural practices of environmentalists present a somewhat paradoxical picture. Culturally speaking, the lifestyle of the average activist is quite coherent with the sought after 'cultural majority'. Politically, *Les Verts* have innovated in certain areas (primaries, mandates, etc.) but their internal political behavior is far from an example of the kind of convivial, participatory society they are, in theory, aiming for. This may be the political 'teething' process that any new movement goes through or the reflection of an individualism which would hinder the collective approach necessary for long term success. Only time will provide the answer to that.

The environmental identity would seem to be now fairly well established. The struggle with the alternative left is over as the latter is in virtual demise and its main spokespersons (e.g. Pierre Juquin, Jean-Paul Deléage) have now joined *Les Verts*. Two thirds of environmentalists have no other political experience before joining an environmental party and a good third do not feel close to any of the major parties. The groundwork for an alternative political culture has been done and now it is a question of bringing together the natural and social strands of the environmental equation.

Somewhat paradoxically, the environmental social base is lacking in diversity with an overwhelming majority of intellectuals. In a society increasingly based on the information sector, this may not necessarily be seen as a disadvantage in the struggle for political power. This situation is, however, in contradiction with the wish of *Les Verts* to create a cultural majority in the French population based on environment-friendly lifestyles. Such a strategy needs openings into each of the different professional categories and the activist typology is a long way from it. The widening of the activist social base would seem to be a priority for environmentalism but not an easy task in a society whose appetite for political activism has waned considerably over the last decade.

In the final analysis, one wonders whether environmentalism is a social movement, a political party, a pressure group or a kind of "environmental trade union" (Allan Michaud 1979: 1045)? Does it matter? For the voters, of course, it does not but for the activists and sympathizers it is a different story as the definition of their situation is a basis for action. That is to say that if environmentalists consider themselves to be simply members of a political party, they only really need to 'oil the electoral wheels', as it were. If, however, they see themselves as actors in a wider social movement which reaches into civil and political society, then the articulation between what we have called the vertical (political society) and horizontal (civil society) axes of the environmental social movement would need reinforcing. The leaders of *Les Verts* seem to be aware of this: "We have to remain in touch with the real world by developing contacts with the associations, but we musn't stifle them in the process" (Christian Brodhag: *Tribune Verte*, N°5, November 1989).

In France, the associationist sector is very wary of politicians and the latter avoid interfering in the former's affairs. The history of the Communist Party's influence over the trade union, the CGT, explains this understandable fear of associations that if they are seen to have close contacts with a political party, they will lose their autonomy. However, this produces a somewhat paradoxical situation. Given the 'objective' identification of environmental associations with the environmentalist political parties (*Les Verts*, *Génération Ecologie*), in the public eye, the former attempt to counter this impression by avoiding the environmentalist parties even more than the traditional parties.

There is no easy solution to the perennial question in political sociology of the relationships between political and civil society. And if there was, environmentalists would, no doubt, be aware of it. Having said that, the end result of this situation is one in which sociopolitical groups working for similar aims, do so separately. Many people believe this to be a more healthy situation in that the associations retain their autonomy. Unfortunately, this autonomy means little if they do not have the sufficient backing in membership terms to influence political decisions and we have seen that, in the area of environmentalism as well as in other areas (e.g. trade unionism), the French public is not very active.

The nature of French society has changed over the last decade. The first, and most important, of these changes was the election of F. Mitterrand which was the cause of widespread sociopolitical demobilization. The vast majority of the left-wing opposition movement of the 1970s then considered that the job was finished and change would come from the top. *Les Verts* suffered, as did others, from an increasing collective lack of interest in politics reinforced by a powerful wave of enterprise culture discourse, which the party in government (i.e. the PS) took fully on board. This context led the environmentalists to concentrate on institutional integration at the expense of their foothold in civil society. The creation of *Les Verts* in 1984 and the first electoral successes of 1989 seemed to justify this strategy. In doing so, however, they leant heavily on a 'naturalist' image of environmentalism. The immediate difficulty for *Les Verts* (and *Génération Ecologie* since 1990), is to demonstrate their will and capacity to deal with the serious business of general politics (e.g. economic, social and international affairs etc.). Their future may depend on it.

The creation of *Génération Ecologie* in 1990 and the rivalry between the two environmental organizations has considerably blurred the picture. *Génération Ecologie* wishes to 'politicize the environment' and *Les Verts* to 'environmentalize politics'. In the middle lies the PS, smarting from its loss of power in 1993, and ready to pick up the confused environmentalist sympathizer with a new, green-tinted programme. Whether the environmentalists will consider a new-look PS as a threat to their existence or the necessary step to future power-sharing is, at the time of writing, *the* question facing French environmentalism.

Appendix 1

Administrative Maps of France

Regions

Departments

Appendix 2

Administrative Regions and Departments of France

Region	Department Name	Dept N°
ALSACE	Bas-Rhin	67
	Haut-Rhin	68
AQUITAINE	Dordogne	24
	Gironde	33
	Landes	40
	Lot-et-Garonne	47
	Pyrénées-Atlantiques	64
AUVERGNE	Allier	03
	Cantal	15
	Haute-Loire	43
	Puy-de-Dôme	63
BOURGOGNE	Côte d'Or	21
	Nièvre	58
	Saône-et-Loire	71
	Yonne	89
BRETAGNE	Côtes du Nord	
	(now Côtes d'Armor)	22
	Finistère	29
	Ille-et-Vilaine	35
	Morbihan	56
CENTRE	Cher	18
	Eure-et-Loir	28
	Indre	36
	Indre-et-Loire	37
	Loir-et-Cher	41
	Loiret	45
CHAMPAGNE-ARDENNES	Ardennes	08
	Aube	10
	Marne	51
	Haute-Marne	52
CORSE	Corse-du-Sud	2A
	Haute-Corse	2B

Region	Department Name	Dept N°
FRANCHE-COMTE	Doubs	25
	Jura	39
	Haute-Saône	70
	Territoire-de-Belfort	90
ILE-DE-FRANCE	Paris	75
	Seine-et-Marne	77
	Yvelines	78
	Essone	91
	Hauts-de-Seine	92
	Seine Saint-Denis	93
	Val-de-Marne	94
	Val d'Oise	95
LANGUEDOC-ROUSILLON	Aude	11
	Gard	30
	Hérault	34
	Lozère	48
	Pyrénées-Orientales	66
LIMOUSIN	Corrèze	19
	Creuse	23
	Haute-Vienne	87
LORRAINE	Meurthe-et-Moselle	54
	Meuse	55
	Moselle	57
	Vosges	88
MIDI-PYRENEES	Ariège	09
	Aveyron	12
	Haute-Garonne	31
	Gers	32
	Lot	46
	Haute-Pyrénées	65
	Tarn	81
	Tarn-et-Garonne	82
NORD-PAS-DE-CALAIS	Nord	59
	Pas-de-Calais	62
BASSE-NORMANDIE	Calvados	14
	Manche	50
	Orne	61
HAUTE-NORMANDIE	Eure	27
	Seine-Maritime	76

Region	Department Name	Dept N°
PAYS DE LA LOIRE	Loire-Atlantique	44
	Maine-et-Loire	49
	Mayenne	53
	Sarthe	72
	Vendée	85
PICARDIE	Aisne	02
	Oise	60
	Somme	80
POITOU-CHARENTES	Charentes	16
	Charente-Maritime	17
	Deux-Sèvres	79
	Vienne	86
PROVENCE-ALPES-COTES D'AZUR		
	Alpes-de-Haute-Provence	04
	Hautes-Alpes	05
	Alpes-Maritimes	06
	Bouches-du-Rhône	13
	Var	83
	Vaucluse	84
RHONE-ALPES	Ain	01
	Ardèche	07
	Drôme	26
	Isère	38
	Loire	42
	Rhône	69
	Savoie	73
	Haute-Savoie	74

Abbreviations and Acronyms

AGM:	*Annual General Meeting*
AJEPNE:	*Association des Journalistes et Ecrivains pour la Protection de la Nature et de l'Environnement*
ALDEA:	*Agence de Liaison pour le Développement des Entreprises Alternatives* (which became *Agence de Liaison pour le Développement d'une Economie Alternative*)
ANRED:	*Agence Nationale pour la Récupération et l'Elimination des Déchets*
APRE:	*Agence de Presse Réhabilitation Ecologique*
APRI:	*Association pour la Protection contre les Rayonnements Ionisants*
AQA:	*Agence pour la Qualité de l'Air*
CDS:	*Centre des Démocrates Sociaux*
CEA:	*Commissariat à l'Energie Atomique*
CFDT:	*Confédération Française Démocratique du Travail*
CGT:	*Confédération Générale du Travail*
CIGALE:	*Club d'Investissement pour la Gestion Alternative de l'Epargne*
CLIN:	*Comité Local d'Information Nucléaire*
CNIR:	*Conseil National Inter-Regional*
CNPF:	*Conseil National du Patronat Français*
CRIN:	*Comité Régional d'Information Nucléaire*
CSFR:	*Comité de Sauvegarde de Fessenheim et de la Plaine du Rhin*
D.D.S.:	*Déçus du socialisme'*
DIREN:	*Directions Régionales de l'Environnement*
DUP:	*Déclaration d'Utilité Publique*
EDF:	*Electricité de France*
ERE:	*Entente-Radicale-Ecologiste*
EUP:	*Enquête d'Utilité Publique*
FEN:	*Fédération de l'Education Nationale*
FFSPN:	*Fédération Française des Sociétés de Protection de la Nature*
FGA:	*Fédération de la Gauche Alternative*
FN:	*Front National*
FNAUT:	*Fédération Nationale des Usagers des Transports*

FNE:	*France-Nature-Environnement*
FNSEA:	*Fédération Nationale des Syndicats d'Exploitants Agricoles*
FNSPN:	*Fédération Nationale des Sociétés de Protection de la Nature*
FO:	*Force Ouvrière*
GE:	*Génération Ecologie*
GSIEN:	*Groupement des Scientifiques pour l'Information sur l'Energie Nucléaire*
HLM:	*Habitation à loyer modéré*
INSEE:	*Institut National de la Statistique et des Etudes Economiques*
IEJE:	*Institut Economique et Juridique de l'Energie*
LCR:	*Ligue Communiste Révolutionnaire*
LPO:	*Ligue pour la Protection des Oiseaux*
MAN:	*Mouvement pour une Alternative Non-Violente*
ME:	*Mouvement Ecologique*
MEP:	*Mouvement d'Ecologie Politique*
MP:	*Member of Parliament (député)*
MIT:	*Massachusett's Institute of Technology*
PSU:	*Parti Socialiste Unifiée*
RAT:	*Réseau des Amis de la Terre*
RIP:	*Référendum d'Initiative Populaire*
RPR:	*Rassemblement Pour la République*
SCPRI:	*Service Central de Protection contre les Rayonnements Ionisants*
SGEN:	*Syndicat Général de l'Education Nationale*
SNES:	*Syndicat National des l'Enseignement Secondaire*
SNI:	*Syndicat National des Instituteurs*
SNPN:	*Société Française de Protection de la Nature*
SOFRES:	*Société Française d'Etudes par Sondages*
UDF:	*Union pour la Démocratie Française*
UPF:	*Union Pour la France*

Bibliography

Dates in brackets [ ] indicate the date of the edition used

ABERCROMBIE Nicholas, HILL Stephen and TURNER Bryan S. 1988. *Dictionary of Sociology.* London: Penguin.

ALLAN MICHAUD Dominique. 1979. *Le discours écologique.* (Certificat International d'Ecologie Humaine). Université de Bordeaux 1. _____. 1989. *L'Avenir de la société alternative.* Paris: L'Harmattan.

ALMOND Gabriel. 1956. "Comparative political systems" in MACRIDIS Roy C. and BROWN Bernard E. (eds.). *Comparative Politics Notes and Readings* (3rd edition). Homewood, Illinois: The Dorsey Press.

ALMOND Gabriel and VERBA Sidney. 1963. *The Civic Culture: Political Attitudes and Democracy in Five Nations.* New Jersey: Princeton University Press.

ALPHANDERY Pierre, BITOUN Pierre and DUPONT Yves. 1991. *L'Equivoque écologique.* Paris: La Découverte.

AUJOURD'HUI L'ECOLOGIE. 1981 (*Ecologie Mensuel*). *Le pouvoir de vivre.* Montargis.

BAHRO Rudolf. 1982. *Socialism and Survival.* London: Heretic Books.

BANKS John A. 1972. *The Sociology of Social Movements.* London: Macmillan.

BARRIER-LYNN Christiane. 1975. "Ecologie, vers un despotisme super éclairé?" in *Esprit.* September.

BAUMAN Zygmunt. 1990. *Thinking Sociologically.* Oxford (GB): Basil Blackwell.

BEAULIEU François de. 1978. *Les dents du progrès.* Paris: Le Sycomore.

BELL Daniel. 1973. *The Coming of the Post-Industrial Society.* New York: Basic Books.

BENEY G. 1990. "Gaïa: de l'hypothèse au mythe" in *Futuribles.* June. Pp. 43-57.

BENNAHMIAS Jean-Luc and ROCHE Agnès. 1992. *Des verts de toutes les couleurs.* Paris: Albin Michel.

BERGER Peter L. 1963. *Invitation to Sociology. A Humanistic Perspective.* New York: Garden City Books.

BERGER Peter L. and KELLNER Hansfried. 1981. *Sociology Reinterpreted.* Middlesex: Pelican.

BLACKWELL Trevor and SEABROOK Jeremy. 1988. *The Politics of Hope.* London: Faber & Faber.

BOGGS Carl. 1976 [1980]. *Gramsci's Marxism.* London: Pluto Press.

BOOKCHIN Murray. 1981. *Toward an Ecological Society*. Montreal: Black Rose Books.

_____. 1982. *The Ecology of Freedom*. Palo Alto: Cheshire Books.

_____. 1987. *The Modern Crisis*. Montreal: Black Rose Books.

_____. 1990. *The Philosophy of Social Ecology*. Montreal: Black Rose Books.

BOY Daniel. 1981. "Le vote écologiste en 1978" in *La Revue Française de Science Politique*. Vol. 32, N°2. April. Pp. 394-416.

_____. 1989. "L'écologisme en France: évolutions et structures" (Workshop: "Political Ecologism: Its Constants and Differences in Europe"). European Consortium for Political Research. *Fondation Nationale des Sciences Politiques*. 10 - 15 April. Paris.

BRAUD Philippe. 1985. *La vie politique*. Paris: P.U.F.

BRIERE Jean. 1982. *Un monde en crise, une planète en péril (Projet de Manifeste du Parti Ecologiste)*. October.

BRIERE Jean. 1984. *Du rouge au vert, au delà de l'utopie révolutionnaire*. (Text). AGM of *Les Verts*. Dijon.

BRODHAG Christian. 1990. *Objectif Terre. Les Verts, de l'écologie à la politique*. Paris: Ed. du Félin.

BROWN Lester. 1989. *The State of The World*. London: W. W. Norton.

BUCHMANN Andrée, HASCOET Guy, MARIMOT Guy and WAECHTER Antoine. 1988. *Motion d'orientation* in *Vert Contact*. N° 82 bis.

BUNYARD P. and MORGAN-GRENVILLE F. (eds.) 1987. *The Green Alternative (Guide to Good Living)*. London: Methuen.

CANS Roger. 1992. *Tous Verts!* Paris: Calmann-Lévy.

CAPRA Fritjof. 1982. *The Turning Point*. London: Fontana.

CARRE Michel, PERRIGUEUX Michèle, MASQUELIER Geneviève and MASSIP Béatrice & Gérard. 1986. *Quel chien dans un jeu de quilles? (Motion d'orientation)*. AGM of *Les Verts*. Paris.

CARSON Rachel. 1965. *Silent Spring*. London: Penguin.

CASTORIADIS Cornelius, COHN-BENDIT Daniel et le public de Louvain La-Neuve. 1981. *De l'écologie à l'autonomie*. Paris: Seuil.

CFDT. 1979. *Energie nucléaire: choisir notre avenir*. Paris: CFDT-Information.

CFDT. 1980. *Le dossier électronucléaire*. Paris: Seuil (Points).

CHAFER Tony. 1982. "The Anti-Nuclear Movement and the Rise of Political Ecology" in P. Cerny (ed.). *Social Movements and Protest in France*. London: Frances Pinter.

_____. 1983 [a]. "The Greens and the Municipal Elections" in *The Review of the Association for the Study of Modern and Contemporary France*. N° 14. May - June. Portsmouth Polytechnic (GB).

————. 1983 [b]. "Interview with Brice Lalonde, 9 February 1983" in *The Review of the Association for the Study of Modern and Contemporary France*. N°14. May - June. Portsmouth Polytechnic (GB).

————. 1984. "The Greens in France: An Emerging Social Movement?" in *The Journal of Area Studies*. N° 10. Portsmouth Polytechnic (GB).

————. 1985. "Politics and the Perception of Risk: a Study of the Anti-Nuclear Movement in Britain and France" in *West European Politics*. Vol. 8. January. Portsmouth Polytechnic (GB).

CHEVALLIER Henry. 1982. *Eléments pour une écologie politique*. Riscle: Ende Doman.

CHIBRET R. P. 1991. *Associations écologiques en France et en Allemagne, une analyse culturelle de la mobilisation collective*. Université Paris 1. (*Doctorat en Sciences Politiques*).

CLERC Denis, LIPIETZ Alain and SATRE-BUISSON Joël .1983. *La crise*. Paris: Syros (Coll. *Alternatives Economiques*).

COCHET Yves, CARRE Michel, DOUCET Jacques, VOYNET Dominique, BOUILLY Nicole, COMMANDEUR René, JOBERT Jean-Claude, MORTREUX Jean-Pierre, COSTA Catherine and MARTIN Dominique. 1983. *Texte d'orientation*. Founding Congress of *Les Verts Confédération Ecologiste* (Besançon: 21 - 23 May 1983).

COCHET Yves. 1984 [a]. "Political ecology in France 1974 - 1984" in *The Journal of Area Studies*. Portsmouth Polytechnic. N° 10. Autumn.

————. 1984 [b]. "Les scores à la loupe" in *Le feu vert*. September.

COLLECTIF ECOLOGISTE. 1977. *Les écologistes présentés par eux-mêmes*. Verviers (Belgique): Flash Actualité MARABOUT.

COLSON Jean-Philippe. 1977. *Le nucléaire sans les Français*. Paris: Maspero.

COMMANDEUR René. 1980. *Mouvement d'écologie politique 2* in *Bulletin du MEP*.

COT Jean-Pierre and MOUNIER Jean-Pierre. 1974. *Pour une sociologie politique*. Paris: Seuil.

DELEAGE Jean-Paul. 1991. *Histoire de l'Ecologie, une science de l'homme et de la nature*. Paris: La Découverte.

DOBSON Andrew. 1990. *Green Political Thought*. London: Harper Collins Academic.

DOMENACH Jean-Marie. 1985. "Mounier Emmanuel" in *Encyclopaedia Universalis*. Paris: Vol. 12.

DUMONT René. 1973. *L'Utopie ou la mort*. Paris: Seuil.

————. 1986. *Les raisons de la colère*. Paris: Editions Entente.

DUPUPET Michel. 1984. *Comprendre l'écologie*. Lyon: Chronique Sociale.

DURKHEIM E. 1896 [1986]. *Les Règles de la méthode sociologique*. Paris: P.U.F.

ECOLO. 1981. *90 Propositions des écologistes*. Namur (Belgique). Ecolo.

EDMA (Encyclopédie du Monde Actuel). 1980. *L'Ecologie*. Paris: Livre de Poche.

EHRLICH Paul. 1971. *La Bombe*. Paris: Fayard.

FAGEN Richard. 1969. *The Transformation of Political Culture in Cuba*. Stanford (California): Stanford University Press.

FERRY Luc. 1992. *Le nouvel ordre écologique*. Paris: Grasset.

FOURNIER Alain. 1986. *"Réflexions"* (Texte). AGM of *Les Verts*. Paris.

GAFFNEY J. 1988. "Le républicanisme dans la culture politique française" in *La Revue Politique et Parlementaire*. May - June.

GALBRAITH John. 1961. *L'Ere de l'abondance*. Paris: Calmann-Lévy.

GORZ André. 1978. *Ecologie et politique*. Paris: Seuil.

_____. 1980. *Adieux au prolétariat*. Paris: Galilée.

_____. 1982. "La reconquête du temps" in *Aujourd'hui*, N°54. March.

HERBELE Rudolph. 1951. *Social Movements (An Introduction to Political Sociology)*. New York: Appleton-Croft.

HOWORTH Jolyon, CHILTON Patricia. 1984. *Defence and Dissent in Contemporary France*. Beckenham (Kent): Croom Helm.

HÜLSBERG W. 1988. *The German Greens. A Social and Political Profile*. London. Verso.

ILLICH Ivan. 1973 [1979]. *Tools for Conviviality*. Glasgow: Fontana/Collins.

ILLICH Ivan. 1971. *Libérer l'avenir*. Paris: Seuil.

_____. 1971 [1979]. *Deschooling Society*. Middlesex: Penguin.

_____. 1974 [1979]. *Energy and et equity*. London: Marion Boyars.

INGLEHART Ronald. 1971. "The Silent Revolution in Europe: Intergenerational Change in Post-Industrial Societies" in *The American Political Science Review*. LLXV, 991-1017.

_____. 1977. *The Silent Revolution: Changing Values and Political Styles among Western Publics*. Princeton: N. J. Princeton University Press.

INSEE. 1987. *Données sociales*. Paris.

_____. 1988, 1989, 1990. *Tableaux de l'économie française*. Paris.

JONAS Hans 1979 [1993]. *Le Principe Responsabilité*. Paris: Cerf.

JOURNES Claude. 1979. "Les idées politiques du mouvement écologiste" in *La Revue Française de Science Politique*. Vol. 29. N°2. April.

KOHN Hans. 1965 [1971]. *Nationalism: Its Meaning and History*. London: D. Van Nostrand Co.

KROPOTKINE Peter. 1899 [1985]. *Fields, Factories and Workshops Tomorrow*. London: Freedom Press.

LAMBERT Yves. 1990. "Le monothéisme des valeurs" in *Le Débat*. N°59. Paris: Gallimard.

LECUYER Philippe. 1986. *Alternatives écologiques (Texte d'orientation)*. AGM of *Les Verts*. Paris.

LEGER D. and HERVIEU B. 1985. "La nature des néo-ruraux" in *Protection de la nature: histoire et idéologie. (De la nature à l'environnement)*. *Actes du Colloque de Florac*. 30 - 31 May. 1985. Paris: L'Harmattan.

LOWE Philip and RUDIG Wolfgang. 1986. "Political Ecology and the Social Sciences -- The State of the Art" in *The British Journal of Political Science*. N° 16. Pp.513-550.

LOVELOCK J. 1986. "Gaia: the world as a living organism" in *The New Scientist*. 18 December.

MANNHEIM Karl. 1943. *Diagnosis of Our Time*. Edinburgh University Press.

MAURICE Antoine. 1987. *Le surfer et le militant*. Paris: Autrement.

MAYER Sylvie. 1990. *Parti pris pour l'écologie*. Paris: Messidor/Editions Sociales.

MEADOWS Denis et al. 1972. *Halte à la croissance*. Paris: Fayard.

MEP (*Mouvement d'écologie politique*) 2. 1980. *Bulletin interne*.

MELUCCI Alberto. 1989. *Nomads of the Present. Social Movements and Individual Needs in Contemporary Society*. London: Hutchinson Radius.

MERTON Robert. 1957. *Social Theory and Social Structure*. New York: Free Press.

_____. 1973. "The self-fulfilling prophecy", in MIZRUCHI H. 1973, *The Substance of Sociology* (2nd Edition). New York: Meredith Corp.

MICHELS Robert. 1911 [1962]. *Political Parties: A Sociological Study of the Oligarchical Tendencies of Modern Democracy*. New York: Free Press.

MORIN Edgar. 1984. *Sociologie*. Paris: Fayard.

_____. 1990. "La Pensée écologisée" in *Le Monde Diplomatique* (Coll. *Manière de voir* 8). May.

MORIN Edgar and KERN Anne Brigitte. 1993. *Terre-Patrie*. Paris: Seuil.

MOSCOVICI Serge. 1985. "Les contradictions de l'écologie" (interview) in *POUR*. N° 99. Pp. 72-75.

MOUNIER Emmanuel. 1949 [1985]. *Le Personnalisme*. Paris: P.U.F.

NELKIN Dorothy and POLLACK Michael. 1982. *The Atom Beseiged*. Massachusetts: MIT.

OBERSCHALL Anthony. 1973. *Social Conflict and Social Movements*. New Jersey: Prentice Hall.

OLSON Mancur. 1971. *The Logic of Collective Action*. New York: Schocken.

PARKIN S. 1989. *Green Parties. An International Guide.* London: Heretic Books.

PATRICK Glenda M. 1978. *"Political Culture": A Conceptual Analysis of the Elements of Political Culture.* World Congress of Sociology. Uppsala, Sweden.

PEPPER David. 1984. *The Roots of Modern Environmentalism.* London: Croom Helm.

PEPPER David. 1985. "Age-old principles", *Green Line.* N°30. March.

_____. 1986. "Radical Environmentalism and the Labour Movement" in Weston (ed.). *Red and Green.* London: Pluto Press.

PORRITT Jonathon. 1984. *Seeing Green.* Oxford: Blackwell.

POTEL Jean-Yves (Direction). 1985. *L'Etat de la France.* Paris: La Découverte.

PRENDIVILLE Brendan. 1981. *Plogoff, Le Pellerin: même combat?.* Rennes: *Les Amis de la Terre.*

_____. 1989. "Les Verts" in F. Müller-Rommel (ed.) *New Politics in Western Europe: The Rise and Success of Green Parties and Alternative Lists.* London: Westview Press.

_____. 1991. *The Political Ecology Movement in France* (Ph.D.). University of Reading (GB).

PRENDIVILLE Brendan and CHAFER Tony. 1989. "The Emergence of the Green Movement in France: Structures and Attitudes within the French Green Movement". (Workshop: *Political Ecologism: Its Constants and Differences in Europe*). European Consortium for Political Research. *Fondation Nationale des Sciences Politiques.* 10 - 15 April. Paris.

PRONIER Raymond and LE SEIGNEUR Vincent Jacques. 1992. *Génération Verte.* Paris: Presses de la Renaissance.

PYE Lucien and VERBA Sidney (eds.). 1965. *Political Culture and Political Development.* New Jersey: Princeton University Press.

RADANNE Pierre. 1987. *Pour une fécondation de l'écologie et du social* (Text of *Arc-en-Ciel*).

RADANNE Pierre and PUISEUX Louis. 1989. *L'énergie dans l'économie.* Paris: Syros/Alternative (Coll. *Alternatives économiques*).

REMY Ronald. 1987. "Transformez votre vie par la pensée positive" in *Evolution: Fédéralisme-Ecologie-Mondialisme.* Revue distributed at the AGM of *Les Verts.* Paris. November.

RENOUVIER Charles. 1984. "Le personnalisme" in *Encyclopaedia Larousse.* Paris. Tome 8.

ROCHE Agnès. 1990. *Résultats du sondage auprès des lecteurs de Vert-Contact.* Paris: *Les Verts.*

ROCHER Guy. 1968. *Introduction à la sociologie générale.* Paris: Seuil.

ROSNAY Joël de. 1975. *Le macroscope.* Paris: Seuil.

RUCHT Dieter. 1987. *Environmental Movement Organisations in West Germany and France* (Unpublished). University of Munich.

SAINTENY Guillaume. 1990. "L'Elite verte. Atypisme provisoire ou préfiguration d'un nouveau personnel politique?" in *Politix*. N°9. Paris: Presses de la Fondation Nationale des Sciences Politiques.

_____. 1991. *Les Verts*. Paris: P.U.F.

_____. 1992. "L'écologisme est-il un centrisme?" in *Libération* (*Collection*). March.

SAMUEL Pierre. 1983. "Une impossibilité gödélienne" in *Combat Nature*. N°56. May - June.

SAVINI Aurélio. 1985. "R.F.A., des banquiers pas comme les autres" in *Alternatives Economiques*. N° 30. October.

SCHUMACHER E. Fritz. 1980. *Small is Beautiful*. London: Abacus.

SEYS Baudouin. 1987. "Les groupes socio-professionnels de 1962 à 1985" in *Données sociales 1987*. Paris: Insee.

SIBILLE Hugues. 1981. "Epargne et développement" in *Alternatives Economiques*. N° 21. March - May.

SIMONNET Dominique. 1979. *L'écologisme*. Paris: P.U.F.

SLATTERY Martin. 1985. *The ABC of Sociology*. London: Macmillan.

SMELSER Neil. 1962. *The Theory of Collective Behaviour*. London: Routledge and Kegan Paul Ltd.

SOFRES. 1989. *Les attitudes politiques des participants à l'assemblée générale écologiste des 18 - 19 November*.

_____. 1990. *Les attitudes politiques des cadres du Parti Socialiste interrogés au congrès de Rennes (-- March -- 1990)*.

TETE Etienne 1987. *Motion d'orientation*. AGM of *Les Verts*. Paris.

THOMAS William I. 1928. *The Child in America. Behaviour Problems and Programs*. New York: Knopf.

TOFFLER Alvin. 1981 [a]. *Future Shock*. London: Pan Books.

_____. 1981 [b]. *The Third Wave*. London: Pan Books.

TOURAINE Alain. 1969. *La société post-industrielle*. Paris: Denoël.

_____. 1980 [a]. *La prophétie anti-nucléaire*. Paris: Seuil.

_____. 1980 [b]. *The Voice and the Eye. An Analysis of Social Movements*. Cambridge (USA): Cambridge University Press.

TOZZI Michel. 1985. *Militer autrement*. Lyon: Chronique Sociale.

_____. 1982. *Syndicalisme et nouveaux mouvements sociaux. Régionalisme, féminisme et écologie*. Lyon: Ed. Ouvrières.

TUCKER Robert C. 1973. "Culture, political culture, communist society" in *Political Science Quarterly* (USA). Vol. 88.

VADROT Claude-Marie. 1978. *L'écologie, histoire d'une subversion*. Paris: Syros.

VIVERET Patrick and ROSANVALLON Pierre. 1977. *Pour une nouvelle culture politique*. Paris: Seuil.

WAECHTER Antoine et al. 1986. *Affirmer l'identité politique des Verts* (Motion). AGM of *Les Verts*. Paris. Supplement to *Vert-Contact*. N°6 1986.

WATTS N. and WANDESFORDE-SMITH G. 1981. "Post-material Values and Evironmental Policy Change" in Lowe and Rudig. 1986.

WEBER Max. 1959. *Le savant et le politique*. Paris: Plon (10/18).

WESTON Joe (ed.). 1986. *Red and Green. The New Politics of the Environment*. London: Pluto Press.

WHITESIDE Kerry. 1992. "The Political Practice of the «Verts»" in *The Review of the Association for the Study of Modern and Contemporary France*. N°48. January. Portsmouth Polytechnic (GB).

WILSON John. 1973. *Introduction to Social Movements*. New York: Basic Books Inc.

Magazines and Newspapers

Libération
Le Monde
Ouest France

Special issues
A FAIRE (ALDEA) 1982. N° 1. November - December.
LA GUEULE OUVERTE 1975. N°80. 19 November.
ECOLOGIE 1981. *L'Ecologie des années 70 - 80...ou 8 ans du journal Ecologie*, N° 335-336-337-338.
LIBERATION (Collection), 1992. *Tout sur les écologistes*. March.
LE MONDE DIPLOMATIQUE (Collection: *Manière de voir* 8) 1990: *La Planète mise à sac*. May.
OBSERVEZ 1992. N°8. March - April 1992.

About the Book and Author

This book analyzes the history and growth of the French environmental movement from its origins in the "back to the earth" wave of the early 1970s to its current influence on every political party from the Trotskyist left to the extreme right of the National Front. In the 1970s, the movement had a libertarian focus, working primarily to spearhead public anti-nuclear sentiment—then the strongest in Europe. However, environmentalists were forced to change their strategies when the socialists came to power in 1981.

Considering the erratic development of the French movement, the author explores the barriers thrown up by France's political culture as well as the nature of the movement's political culture and the role of militants within it. He assesses the ideological sources of French environmentalism, especially important at a time when its platform is becoming an electoral threat that is also open to attacks of ecofascism.

Brendan Prendiville is lecturer in sociology at the University of Rennes 2, Brittany, France, where he has lived since 1978. He received his doctorate from the University of Reading. His interest in environmental politics stems from his long-term study of new social movements in France. He is the author of *L'Ecologie, la politique autrement?* (Paris, 1993).

Index